MENTAL
HEALTH
TRACKER

MENTAL HEALTH TRACKER

A DAILY JOURNAL TO MANAGE ANXIETY AND CREATE HEALTHY HABITS

Zeitgeist • New York

Published in the United States by Zeitgeist, an imprint of Zeitgeist™,
a division of Penguin Random House LLC, New York.
penguinrandomhouse.com

Zeitgeist™ is a trademark of Penguin Random House LLC

ISBN: 9780593435571

Cover design by Whalen Books
Interior design by Katy Brown

Printed in the United States of America
1 3 5 7 9 10 8 6 4 2

First Edition

This journal belongs to

Jessica   Poulten

START WHERE YOU ARE

At one point or another, all of us experience anxious thoughts and feelings. Learning to cope with them is no small task, especially if they start to take over our daily lives and mental health. Now more than ever, anxiety is incredibly common among people of all ages, and it can be triggered by anything from past or present relationships to work and finances to the not-so-simple state of the world.

Everyone experiences it, and yet anxiety can feel incredibly isolating, as if you're the only one going through it. The fact is, though, you are not alone with your worried thoughts. Anxiety is a part of life, and by picking up this journal, you are taking an important first step toward better mental health. In these pages, you'll have the opportunity every day to quickly jot down what's coming up for you, and you'll also have a chance to look back once a month to see if you can spot any trends around triggers and what's working (and what isn't). Let this journal be your guide to understanding and living with your thoughts and feelings.

If you are having a hard time managing your anxiety (especially if it is interfering with day-to-day life), consider reaching out to loved ones who care for you deeply or working with an experienced therapist.

THE POWER OF TRACKING

Logging your daily thoughts, triggers, and self-care habits can help you become more in tune with your feelings and anxiety and in turn improve your mental well-being. This journal provides 24 weeks' worth of daily tracking so you can touch base with yourself and your mood throughout the day, plus 6 monthly check-ins to reflect back on what you've gathered in the dailies and see if there are any actions you want to increase or decrease.

More than anything, it's important to go at your own pace, and remember that it's OK to only fill out what you think is most helpful to you at the start. As you get into a groove of daily tracking, you may find that eventually you want to complete more and more of the prompts found on the daily log pages.

The Good News

Tracking your feelings and anxiety is like any other skill—once you start, it only gets easier. It's also an ongoing process toward better mental health. As you fill out this journal, remember:

- There are no rules. This journal is a reflection of you; write about whatever you want.
- Journaling is not a chore. It is an opportunity to reflect, cope, and grow.
- Try not to censor your thoughts—these pages are a safe and private space, so be honest with yourself.
- Most importantly, give yourself credit. You are bettering yourself every time you reach for this book.
- Take the time to celebrate your progress, both big and small. There is no immediate, magical fix for anxiety. Improvement takes time, so if you become impatient or start labeling something as a setback, take a deep breath and remind yourself that even baby steps will lead a person on a path toward peace and happiness.

DAILY TRACKER

Jot down things as they come up throughout the day, or find time in the morning or evening where you can take a few minutes to write. Honor whatever truly works for you, and you're more likely to look forward to using these pages.

For each day, you'll find prompts for recording up to three notable feelings that present themselves, as well as self-care checklists and a fill-in-the-blank gratitude journaling space as a reminder of what's important to you. There's no right or wrong way to go about it, but the following information provides a quick guide to the daily log pages.

Time: Each daily log has space for recording up to three notable moments or feelings that show up. By marking the time of day they happen, you may later be able to pick up on a pattern.

Feeling: Anger? Sadness? Joy? Whatever it is you're feeling, name it.

Intensity: On a scale of 1 to 10, how big does this feeling present?

Situation: Describe what led up to this feeling. It could be a conversation, a particular environment, or even thoughts you were having right before.

Reactions/Strategy: Use this space to record any physical reactions, thoughts, or decisions you made based on this feeling—or what strategy you used to cope with the feeling. Was it successful?

Anxiety Level After: On a scale of 1 to 10, rate your anxiety level. This is different than the intensity of the feeling that kicked everything off; it's a check-in on your overall anxiety level and the impact the named feeling, situation, and reaction/strategy had on it.

Hours Slept: Sleep has been shown to influence mood in the short and long term. Track your hours here.

Nourishment: On a scale of 1 to 10, rate your eating habits today in terms of what ultimately makes you feel nourished, energized, and healthy.

Water: Good hydration can have a whole cascading effect on health, mood, and stamina. Note how many glasses, ounces, or bottles of water you drank.

Physical Activity: Increasing heart rate and circulation can come in many forms and is a proven mood-booster. This is a mental health goal, not a weight-loss tactic.

Other: Personalize this as you like. Or, if you're aiming to change one thing or try a new health habit this month, note if you worked on it today. (If not, there's always tomorrow.)

Impact on Mood: Yes or no, did any self-care make a difference today?

WHAT HAPPENED TODAY

M| *Nov*   D| *9*   Y| *2021*

TIME: *8:15 am*   FEELING: *Mad*   INTENSITY (1-10): *4*

SITUATION: *Checked email at breakfast.*

REACTION/STRATEGY: *Ate chocolate after my toast and coffee.*

ANXIETY LEVEL AFTER (1-10): *5*

TIME: *11:30am*   FEELING: *Happy*   INTENSITY (1-10): *6*

SITUATION: *Rode bike for 30 min.*

REACTION/STRATEGY: *Physical activity to clear brain.*

ANXIETY LEVEL AFTER (1-10): *2*

TIME: *3:45pm*   FEELING: *Stressed*   INTENSITY (1-10): *7*

SITUATION: *Bad meeting with boss.*

REACTION/STRATEGY: *Cried after and ignored the rest of my work.*

ANXIETY LEVEL AFTER (1-10): *8*

Self-Care

HOURS SLEPT: *7 1/2*

NOURISHMENT (1-10): *8*

WATER: *70 oz.*

PHYSICAL ACTIVITY: *30 min. bike ride*

OTHER: *Meditated for 10 min.*

IMPACT ON MOOD (Y/N): *Y for a short time*

Today, I am grateful for:

Having a partner who's so patient and willing to listen to me vent.

MONTHLY CHECK-IN

Every 4 weeks or so, take a moment to observe the past month's worth of daily tracking pages. Look back over the entries, and then reflect on any common themes, feelings, strategies, or self-care habits that seemed to have made an impact. Again, use this space as it best suits you when looking back and making an action plan for the next few weeks. Here are some tips to help you navigate the check-ins.

Average Anxiety Level: Grab a calculator to add up your anxiety level ratings from the past month and divide by the number of days you've recorded. (If you've filled out each of the daily logs, you'll divide by 28.)

2 Most Common Feelings: Record which feelings came up over and over again in your dailies.

What Led Up to the Feeling: If you see one or more patterns in the situations surrounding a feeling, name them here.

Strategies That Worked or Didn't Work: For each item, circle the arrow that reflects the strategy's impact on your mood and anxiety. If it was positive, circle the upward arrow; if it was negative, circle the downward arrow; for neutral, circle the sideways arrow. Then you can decide if you want to increase or decrease the use of that strategy in the future.

Self-Care That Helped Overall Mental Health: For each item, circle the arrow that reflects your plan for increasing, decreasing, or staying the course with this self-care activity if you noticed it led to better moods.

For Next Month: If you like, pick one thing you want to focus on doing differently or a value you'd like to focus on over the next four weeks. Then briefly spell out how you plan to do it.

Sample Entry

WHAT HAPPENED THIS MONTH   M| *Nov*   Y| *2021*

Average Anxiety Level

① ② ③ ④ ⑤ ⑥ ⑦ ⑧ ⑨ ⑩

2 Most Common Feelings

Sad

Worried

↓   WHAT LED UP TO THE FEELING   ↓

- Usually, not getting enough
  sleep 2+ days in a row

- Group meetings over Zoom
- Looking at social media

↓   STRATEGIES THAT WORKED OR DIDN'T WORK   ↓

⊙↓↔ Having a last cup of
  coffee right after lunch

↑↓☺ Going to bed 30 min.
  early

⊙↓↔ LED therapy lights

↑↓☺ Contributing over Zoom's
  chat instead of speaking

⊙↓↔ Limiting my social
  media time to 10 min/day

↑↓↔

Self-Care That Helped Overall Mental Health

⊙↓↔ 10 minutes of bedtime meditation app

↑↓☺ Taking a walk every morning

↑⊙↔ 21 days without sugar

For Next Month

I WANT TO FOCUS ON CHANGING ONE THING: Increasing my energy during
the day to combat sadness.

THIS IS HOW I'LL DO IT: I'm going to add a 15-minute walk or bike
ride after lunch.

WHAT HAPPENED TODAY

M| D| Y|

TIME: 7:45   FEELING: Sad/Sick   INTENSITY (1–10): 8

SITUATION: I caught the stomache bug going around school.

REACTION/STRATEGY: Get better

ANXIETY LEVEL AFTER (1–10): 7

TIME: FEELING: INTENSITY (1–10):

SITUATION:

REACTION/STRATEGY:

ANXIETY LEVEL AFTER (1–10):

TIME: FEELING: INTENSITY (1–10):

SITUATION:

REACTION/STRATEGY:

ANXIETY LEVEL AFTER (1–10):

Self-Care

HOURS SLEPT:

NOURISHMENT (1-10):

WATER:

PHYSICAL ACTIVITY:

OTHER:

IMPACT ON MOOD (Y/N):

Today, I am grateful for:

| M| | D| | Y| |

WHAT HAPPENED TODAY

TIME: .... FEELING: .... INTENSITY (1–10): ....

SITUATION: ....

REACTION/STRATEGY: ....

ANXIETY LEVEL AFTER (1–10): ....

TIME: .... FEELING: .... INTENSITY (1–10): ....

SITUATION: ....

REACTION/STRATEGY: ....

ANXIETY LEVEL AFTER (1–10): ....

TIME: .... FEELING: .... INTENSITY (1–10): ....

SITUATION: ....

REACTION/STRATEGY: ....

ANXIETY LEVEL AFTER (1–10): ....

Self-Care

HOURS SLEPT: ....

NOURISHMENT (1-10): ....

WATER: ....

PHYSICAL ACTIVITY: ....

OTHER: ....

IMPACT ON MOOD (Y/N): ....

Today, I am grateful for:

WHAT HAPPENED TODAY

M| D| Y|

TIME: FEELING: INTENSITY (1–10):

SITUATION:

REACTION/STRATEGY:

ANXIETY LEVEL AFTER (1–10):

TIME: FEELING: INTENSITY (1–10):

SITUATION:

REACTION/STRATEGY:

ANXIETY LEVEL AFTER (1–10):

TIME: FEELING: INTENSITY (1–10):

SITUATION:

REACTION/STRATEGY:

ANXIETY LEVEL AFTER (1–10):

Self-Care

HOURS SLEPT:

NOURISHMENT (1-10):

WATER:

PHYSICAL ACTIVITY:

OTHER:

IMPACT ON MOOD (Y/N):

Today, I am grateful for:

| M| | D| | Y| |

WHAT HAPPENED TODAY

TIME: FEELING: INTENSITY (1-10):

SITUATION:

REACTION/STRATEGY:

ANXIETY LEVEL AFTER (1-10):

TIME: FEELING: INTENSITY (1-10):

SITUATION:

REACTION/STRATEGY:

ANXIETY LEVEL AFTER (1-10):

TIME: FEELING: INTENSITY (1-10):

SITUATION:

REACTION/STRATEGY:

ANXIETY LEVEL AFTER (1-10):

Self-Care

HOURS SLEPT:

NOURISHMENT (1-10):

WATER:

PHYSICAL ACTIVITY:

OTHER:

IMPACT ON MOOD (Y/N):

Today, I am grateful for:

WHAT HAPPENED TODAY

M| D| Y|

TIME: FEELING: INTENSITY (1–10):

SITUATION:

REACTION/STRATEGY:

ANXIETY LEVEL AFTER (1–10):

TIME: FEELING: INTENSITY (1–10):

SITUATION:

REACTION/STRATEGY:

ANXIETY LEVEL AFTER (1–10):

TIME: FEELING: INTENSITY (1–10):

SITUATION:

REACTION/STRATEGY:

ANXIETY LEVEL AFTER (1–10):

Self-Care

HOURS SLEPT:

NOURISHMENT (1-10):

WATER:

PHYSICAL ACTIVITY:

OTHER:

IMPACT ON MOOD (Y/N):

Today, I am grateful for:

| M| | D| | Y| |

WHAT HAPPENED TODAY

TIME: FEELING: INTENSITY (1–10):

SITUATION:

REACTION/STRATEGY:

ANXIETY LEVEL AFTER (1–10):

TIME: FEELING: INTENSITY (1–10):

SITUATION:

REACTION/STRATEGY:

ANXIETY LEVEL AFTER (1–10):

TIME: FEELING: INTENSITY (1–10):

SITUATION:

REACTION/STRATEGY:

ANXIETY LEVEL AFTER (1–10):

Self-Care

HOURS SLEPT:

NOURISHMENT (1-10):

WATER:

PHYSICAL ACTIVITY:

OTHER:

IMPACT ON MOOD (Y/N):

Today, I am grateful for:

WHAT HAPPENED TODAY

M| D| Y|

TIME: FEELING: INTENSITY (1–10):

SITUATION:

REACTION/STRATEGY:

ANXIETY LEVEL AFTER (1–10):

TIME: FEELING: INTENSITY (1–10):

SITUATION:

REACTION/STRATEGY:

ANXIETY LEVEL AFTER (1–10):

TIME: FEELING: INTENSITY (1–10):

SITUATION:

REACTION/STRATEGY:

ANXIETY LEVEL AFTER (1–10):

Self-Care

HOURS SLEPT:

NOURISHMENT (1-10):

WATER:

PHYSICAL ACTIVITY:

OTHER:

IMPACT ON MOOD (Y/N):

Today, I am grateful for:

M| D| Y|

WHAT HAPPENED TODAY

TIME: FEELING: INTENSITY (1–10):

SITUATION:

REACTION/STRATEGY:

ANXIETY LEVEL AFTER (1–10):

TIME: FEELING: INTENSITY (1–10):

SITUATION:

REACTION/STRATEGY:

ANXIETY LEVEL AFTER (1–10):

TIME: FEELING: INTENSITY (1–10):

SITUATION:

REACTION/STRATEGY:

ANXIETY LEVEL AFTER (1–10):

Self-Care

HOURS SLEPT:

NOURISHMENT (1-10):

WATER:

PHYSICAL ACTIVITY:

OTHER:

IMPACT ON MOOD (Y/N):

Today, I am grateful for:

WHAT HAPPENED TODAY

M| D| Y|

TIME: FEELING: INTENSITY (1-10):

SITUATION:

REACTION/STRATEGY:

ANXIETY LEVEL AFTER (1-10):

TIME: FEELING: INTENSITY (1-10):

SITUATION:

REACTION/STRATEGY:

ANXIETY LEVEL AFTER (1-10):

TIME: FEELING: INTENSITY (1-10):

SITUATION:

REACTION/STRATEGY:

ANXIETY LEVEL AFTER (1-10):

Self-Care

HOURS SLEPT:

NOURISHMENT (1-10):

WATER:

PHYSICAL ACTIVITY:

OTHER:

IMPACT ON MOOD (Y/N):

Today, I am grateful for:

WHAT HAPPENED TODAY

TIME: FEELING: INTENSITY (1–10):

SITUATION:

REACTION/STRATEGY:

ANXIETY LEVEL AFTER (1–10):

TIME: FEELING: INTENSITY (1–10):

SITUATION:

REACTION/STRATEGY:

ANXIETY LEVEL AFTER (1–10):

TIME: FEELING: INTENSITY (1–10):

SITUATION:

REACTION/STRATEGY:

ANXIETY LEVEL AFTER (1–10):

Self-Care

HOURS SLEPT:

NOURISHMENT (1-10):

WATER:

PHYSICAL ACTIVITY:

OTHER:

IMPACT ON MOOD (Y/N):

Today, I am grateful for:

WHAT HAPPENED TODAY

M| D| Y|

TIME: FEELING: INTENSITY (1–10):

SITUATION:

REACTION/STRATEGY:

ANXIETY LEVEL AFTER (1–10):

TIME: FEELING: INTENSITY (1–10):

SITUATION:

REACTION/STRATEGY:

ANXIETY LEVEL AFTER (1–10):

TIME: FEELING: INTENSITY (1–10):

SITUATION:

REACTION/STRATEGY:

ANXIETY LEVEL AFTER (1–10):

Self-Care

HOURS SLEPT:

NOURISHMENT (1-10):

WATER:

PHYSICAL ACTIVITY:

OTHER:

IMPACT ON MOOD (Y/N):

Today, I am grateful for:

| M| | D| | Y| |

WHAT HAPPENED TODAY

TIME: FEELING: INTENSITY (1–10):

SITUATION:

REACTION/STRATEGY:

ANXIETY LEVEL AFTER (1–10):

TIME: FEELING: INTENSITY (1–10):

SITUATION:

REACTION/STRATEGY:

ANXIETY LEVEL AFTER (1–10):

TIME: FEELING: INTENSITY (1–10):

SITUATION:

REACTION/STRATEGY:

ANXIETY LEVEL AFTER (1–10):

Self-Care

HOURS SLEPT:

NOURISHMENT (1-10):

WATER:

PHYSICAL ACTIVITY:

OTHER:

IMPACT ON MOOD (Y/N):

Today, I am grateful for:

WHAT HAPPENED TODAY

M| D| Y|

TIME: _____ FEELING: _____ INTENSITY (1–10): _____

SITUATION: _____

REACTION/STRATEGY: _____

ANXIETY LEVEL AFTER (1–10): _____

TIME: _____ FEELING: _____ INTENSITY (1–10): _____

SITUATION: _____

REACTION/STRATEGY: _____

ANXIETY LEVEL AFTER (1–10): _____

TIME: _____ FEELING: _____ INTENSITY (1–10): _____

SITUATION: _____

REACTION/STRATEGY: _____

ANXIETY LEVEL AFTER (1–10): _____

Self-Care

HOURS SLEPT: _____

NOURISHMENT (1-10): _____

WATER: _____

PHYSICAL ACTIVITY: _____

OTHER: _____

IMPACT ON MOOD (Y/N): _____

Today, I am grateful for:

WHAT HAPPENED TODAY

TIME: FEELING: INTENSITY (1–10):

SITUATION:

REACTION/STRATEGY:

ANXIETY LEVEL AFTER (1–10):

TIME: FEELING: INTENSITY (1–10):

SITUATION:

REACTION/STRATEGY:

ANXIETY LEVEL AFTER (1–10):

TIME: FEELING: INTENSITY (1–10):

SITUATION:

REACTION/STRATEGY:

ANXIETY LEVEL AFTER (1–10):

Self-Care

HOURS SLEPT:

NOURISHMENT (1-10):

WATER:

PHYSICAL ACTIVITY:

OTHER:

IMPACT ON MOOD (Y/N):

Today, I am grateful for:

WHAT HAPPENED TODAY

M| D| Y|

TIME: FEELING: INTENSITY (1–10):

SITUATION:

REACTION/STRATEGY:

ANXIETY LEVEL AFTER (1–10):

TIME: FEELING: INTENSITY (1–10):

SITUATION:

REACTION/STRATEGY:

ANXIETY LEVEL AFTER (1–10):

TIME: FEELING: INTENSITY (1–10):

SITUATION:

REACTION/STRATEGY:

ANXIETY LEVEL AFTER (1–10):

Self-Care   **Today, I am grateful for:**

HOURS SLEPT:

NOURISHMENT (1-10):

WATER:

PHYSICAL ACTIVITY:

OTHER:

IMPACT ON MOOD (Y/N):

WHAT HAPPENED TODAY

TIME: FEELING: INTENSITY (1–10):

SITUATION:

REACTION/STRATEGY:

ANXIETY LEVEL AFTER (1–10):

TIME: FEELING: INTENSITY (1–10):

SITUATION:

REACTION/STRATEGY:

ANXIETY LEVEL AFTER (1–10):

TIME: FEELING: INTENSITY (1–10):

SITUATION:

REACTION/STRATEGY:

ANXIETY LEVEL AFTER (1–10):

Self-Care

HOURS SLEPT:

NOURISHMENT (1-10):

WATER:

PHYSICAL ACTIVITY:

OTHER:

IMPACT ON MOOD (Y/N):

Today, I am grateful for:

WHAT HAPPENED TODAY

M| D| Y|

TIME: FEELING: INTENSITY (1–10):

SITUATION:

REACTION/STRATEGY:

ANXIETY LEVEL AFTER (1–10):

TIME: FEELING: INTENSITY (1–10):

SITUATION:

REACTION/STRATEGY:

ANXIETY LEVEL AFTER (1–10):

TIME: FEELING: INTENSITY (1–10):

SITUATION:

REACTION/STRATEGY:

ANXIETY LEVEL AFTER (1–10):

Self-Care

HOURS SLEPT:

NOURISHMENT (1-10):

WATER:

PHYSICAL ACTIVITY:

OTHER:

IMPACT ON MOOD (Y/N):

Today, I am grateful for:

WHAT HAPPENED TODAY

TIME: FEELING: INTENSITY (1-10):

SITUATION:

REACTION/STRATEGY:

ANXIETY LEVEL AFTER (1-10):

TIME: FEELING: INTENSITY (1-10):

SITUATION:

REACTION/STRATEGY:

ANXIETY LEVEL AFTER (1-10):

TIME: FEELING: INTENSITY (1-10):

SITUATION:

REACTION/STRATEGY:

ANXIETY LEVEL AFTER (1-10):

Self-Care

HOURS SLEPT:

NOURISHMENT (1-10):

WATER:

PHYSICAL ACTIVITY:

OTHER:

IMPACT ON MOOD (Y/N):

Today, I am grateful for:

WHAT HAPPENED TODAY

M| D| Y|

TIME: FEELING: INTENSITY (1–10):

SITUATION:

REACTION/STRATEGY:

ANXIETY LEVEL AFTER (1–10):

TIME: FEELING: INTENSITY (1–10):

SITUATION:

REACTION/STRATEGY:

ANXIETY LEVEL AFTER (1–10):

TIME: FEELING: INTENSITY (1–10):

SITUATION:

REACTION/STRATEGY:

ANXIETY LEVEL AFTER (1–10):

Self-Care

HOURS SLEPT:

NOURISHMENT (1-10):

WATER:

PHYSICAL ACTIVITY:

OTHER:

IMPACT ON MOOD (Y/N):

Today, I am grateful for:

| M| | D| | Y| |

WHAT HAPPENED TODAY

TIME: FEELING: INTENSITY (1–10):

SITUATION:

REACTION/STRATEGY:

ANXIETY LEVEL AFTER (1–10):

TIME: FEELING: INTENSITY (1–10):

SITUATION:

REACTION/STRATEGY:

ANXIETY LEVEL AFTER (1–10):

TIME: FEELING: INTENSITY (1–10):

SITUATION:

REACTION/STRATEGY:

ANXIETY LEVEL AFTER (1–10):

Self-Care

HOURS SLEPT:

NOURISHMENT (1-10):

WATER:

PHYSICAL ACTIVITY:

OTHER:

IMPACT ON MOOD (Y/N):

Today, I am grateful for:

WHAT HAPPENED TODAY

M| D| Y|

TIME: FEELING: INTENSITY (1–10):

SITUATION:

REACTION/STRATEGY:

ANXIETY LEVEL AFTER (1–10):

TIME: FEELING: INTENSITY (1–10):

SITUATION:

REACTION/STRATEGY:

ANXIETY LEVEL AFTER (1–10):

TIME: FEELING: INTENSITY (1–10):

SITUATION:

REACTION/STRATEGY:

ANXIETY LEVEL AFTER (1–10):

Self-Care

HOURS SLEPT:

NOURISHMENT (1-10):

WATER:

PHYSICAL ACTIVITY:

OTHER:

IMPACT ON MOOD (Y/N):

Today, I am grateful for:

M| D| Y|

WHAT HAPPENED TODAY

TIME: FEELING: INTENSITY (1–10):

SITUATION:

REACTION/STRATEGY:

ANXIETY LEVEL AFTER (1–10):

TIME: FEELING: INTENSITY (1–10):

SITUATION:

REACTION/STRATEGY:

ANXIETY LEVEL AFTER (1–10):

TIME: FEELING: INTENSITY (1–10):

SITUATION:

REACTION/STRATEGY:

ANXIETY LEVEL AFTER (1–10):

Self-Care

HOURS SLEPT:

NOURISHMENT (1-10):

WATER:

PHYSICAL ACTIVITY:

OTHER:

IMPACT ON MOOD (Y/N):

Today, I am grateful for:

WHAT HAPPENED TODAY

M| D| Y|

TIME: FEELING: INTENSITY (1–10):

SITUATION:

REACTION/STRATEGY:

ANXIETY LEVEL AFTER (1–10):

TIME: FEELING: INTENSITY (1–10):

SITUATION:

REACTION/STRATEGY:

ANXIETY LEVEL AFTER (1–10):

TIME: FEELING: INTENSITY (1–10):

SITUATION:

REACTION/STRATEGY:

ANXIETY LEVEL AFTER (1–10):

Self-Care

HOURS SLEPT:

NOURISHMENT (1-10):

WATER:

PHYSICAL ACTIVITY:

OTHER:

IMPACT ON MOOD (Y/N):

Today, I am grateful for:

| M| | D| | Y| |

WHAT HAPPENED TODAY

TIME: FEELING: INTENSITY (1–10):

SITUATION:

REACTION/STRATEGY:

ANXIETY LEVEL AFTER (1–10):

TIME: FEELING: INTENSITY (1–10):

SITUATION:

REACTION/STRATEGY:

ANXIETY LEVEL AFTER (1–10):

TIME: FEELING: INTENSITY (1–10):

SITUATION:

REACTION/STRATEGY:

ANXIETY LEVEL AFTER (1–10):

Self-Care

HOURS SLEPT:

NOURISHMENT (1-10):

WATER:

PHYSICAL ACTIVITY:

OTHER:

IMPACT ON MOOD (Y/N):

Today, I am grateful for:

WHAT HAPPENED TODAY

M| D| Y|

TIME: FEELING: INTENSITY (1–10):

SITUATION:

REACTION/STRATEGY:

ANXIETY LEVEL AFTER (1–10):

TIME: FEELING: INTENSITY (1–10):

SITUATION:

REACTION/STRATEGY:

ANXIETY LEVEL AFTER (1–10):

TIME: FEELING: INTENSITY (1–10):

SITUATION:

REACTION/STRATEGY:

ANXIETY LEVEL AFTER (1–10):

Self-Care

HOURS SLEPT:

NOURISHMENT (1-10):

WATER:

PHYSICAL ACTIVITY:

OTHER:

IMPACT ON MOOD (Y/N):

Today, I am grateful for:

M| D| Y|

WHAT HAPPENED TODAY

TIME: FEELING: INTENSITY (1–10):

SITUATION:

REACTION/STRATEGY:

ANXIETY LEVEL AFTER (1–10):

TIME: FEELING: INTENSITY (1–10):

SITUATION:

REACTION/STRATEGY:

ANXIETY LEVEL AFTER (1–10):

TIME: FEELING: INTENSITY (1–10):

SITUATION:

REACTION/STRATEGY:

ANXIETY LEVEL AFTER (1–10):

Self-Care

HOURS SLEPT:

NOURISHMENT (1-10):

WATER:

PHYSICAL ACTIVITY:

OTHER:

IMPACT ON MOOD (Y/N):

Today, I am grateful for:

WHAT HAPPENED TODAY

M| D| Y|

TIME: FEELING: INTENSITY (1–10):

SITUATION:

REACTION/STRATEGY:

ANXIETY LEVEL AFTER (1–10):

TIME: FEELING: INTENSITY (1–10):

SITUATION:

REACTION/STRATEGY:

ANXIETY LEVEL AFTER (1–10):

TIME: FEELING: INTENSITY (1–10):

SITUATION:

REACTION/STRATEGY:

ANXIETY LEVEL AFTER (1–10):

Self-Care

HOURS SLEPT:

NOURISHMENT (1-10):

WATER:

PHYSICAL ACTIVITY:

OTHER:

IMPACT ON MOOD (Y/N):

Today, I am grateful for:

| M| | D| | Y| |

WHAT HAPPENED TODAY

TIME: FEELING: INTENSITY (1–10):

SITUATION:

REACTION/STRATEGY:

ANXIETY LEVEL AFTER (1–10):

TIME: FEELING: INTENSITY (1–10):

SITUATION:

REACTION/STRATEGY:

ANXIETY LEVEL AFTER (1–10):

TIME: FEELING: INTENSITY (1–10):

SITUATION:

REACTION/STRATEGY:

ANXIETY LEVEL AFTER (1–10):

Self-Care

HOURS SLEPT:

NOURISHMENT (1-10):

WATER:

PHYSICAL ACTIVITY:

OTHER:

IMPACT ON MOOD (Y/N):

Today, I am grateful for:

Average Anxiety Level

① ② ③ ④ ⑤ ⑥ ⑦ ⑧ ⑨ ⑩

2 Most Common Feelings

↓ WHAT LED UP TO THE FEELING ↓

↓ STRATEGIES THAT WORKED OR DIDN'T WORK ↓

↑ ↓ ↔   ↑ ↓ ↔

↑ ↓ ↔   ↑ ↓ ↔

↑ ↓ ↔   ↑ ↓ ↔

Self-Care That Helped Overall Mental Health

↑ ↓ ↔

↑ ↓ ↔

↑ ↓ ↔

For Next Month

I WANT TO FOCUS ON CHANGING ONE THING:

THIS IS HOW I'LL DO IT:

Other Notes and Observations

WHAT HAPPENED TODAY

M| D| Y|

TIME: FEELING: INTENSITY (1–10):

SITUATION:

REACTION/STRATEGY:

ANXIETY LEVEL AFTER (1–10):

TIME: FEELING: INTENSITY (1–10):

SITUATION:

REACTION/STRATEGY:

ANXIETY LEVEL AFTER (1–10):

TIME: FEELING: INTENSITY (1–10):

SITUATION:

REACTION/STRATEGY:

ANXIETY LEVEL AFTER (1–10):

Self-Care

HOURS SLEPT:

NOURISHMENT (1-10):

WATER:

PHYSICAL ACTIVITY:

OTHER:

IMPACT ON MOOD (Y/N):

Today, I am grateful for:

| M| | D| | Y| |

WHAT HAPPENED TODAY

TIME: FEELING: INTENSITY (1–10):

SITUATION:

REACTION/STRATEGY:

ANXIETY LEVEL AFTER (1–10):

TIME: FEELING: INTENSITY (1–10):

SITUATION:

REACTION/STRATEGY:

ANXIETY LEVEL AFTER (1–10):

TIME: FEELING: INTENSITY (1–10):

SITUATION:

REACTION/STRATEGY:

ANXIETY LEVEL AFTER (1–10):

Self-Care

HOURS SLEPT:

NOURISHMENT (1-10):

WATER:

PHYSICAL ACTIVITY:

OTHER:

IMPACT ON MOOD (Y/N):

Today, I am grateful for:

WHAT HAPPENED TODAY

M| D| Y|

TIME: FEELING: INTENSITY (1–10):

SITUATION:

REACTION/STRATEGY:

ANXIETY LEVEL AFTER (1–10):

TIME: FEELING: INTENSITY (1–10):

SITUATION:

REACTION/STRATEGY:

ANXIETY LEVEL AFTER (1–10):

TIME: FEELING: INTENSITY (1–10):

SITUATION:

REACTION/STRATEGY:

ANXIETY LEVEL AFTER (1–10):

Self-Care

HOURS SLEPT:

NOURISHMENT (1-10):

WATER:

PHYSICAL ACTIVITY:

OTHER:

IMPACT ON MOOD (Y/N):

Today, I am grateful for:

| M| | D| | Y| |

WHAT HAPPENED TODAY

TIME: FEELING: INTENSITY (1–10):

SITUATION:

REACTION/STRATEGY:

ANXIETY LEVEL AFTER (1–10):

TIME: FEELING: INTENSITY (1–10):

SITUATION:

REACTION/STRATEGY:

ANXIETY LEVEL AFTER (1–10):

TIME: FEELING: INTENSITY (1–10):

SITUATION:

REACTION/STRATEGY:

ANXIETY LEVEL AFTER (1–10):

Self-Care

HOURS SLEPT:

NOURISHMENT (1-10):

WATER:

PHYSICAL ACTIVITY:

OTHER:

IMPACT ON MOOD (Y/N):

Today, I am grateful for:

WHAT HAPPENED TODAY

M| D| Y|

TIME: FEELING: INTENSITY (1-10):

SITUATION:

REACTION/STRATEGY:

ANXIETY LEVEL AFTER (1-10):

TIME: FEELING: INTENSITY (1-10):

SITUATION:

REACTION/STRATEGY:

ANXIETY LEVEL AFTER (1-10):

TIME: FEELING: INTENSITY (1-10):

SITUATION:

REACTION/STRATEGY:

ANXIETY LEVEL AFTER (1-10):

Self-Care

HOURS SLEPT:

NOURISHMENT (1-10):

WATER:

PHYSICAL ACTIVITY:

OTHER:

IMPACT ON MOOD (Y/N):

Today, I am grateful for:

WHAT HAPPENED TODAY

TIME: FEELING: INTENSITY (1–10):

SITUATION:

REACTION/STRATEGY:

ANXIETY LEVEL AFTER (1–10):

TIME: FEELING: INTENSITY (1–10):

SITUATION:

REACTION/STRATEGY:

ANXIETY LEVEL AFTER (1–10):

TIME: FEELING: INTENSITY (1–10):

SITUATION:

REACTION/STRATEGY:

ANXIETY LEVEL AFTER (1–10):

Self-Care

HOURS SLEPT:

NOURISHMENT (1-10):

WATER:

PHYSICAL ACTIVITY:

OTHER:

IMPACT ON MOOD (Y/N):

Today, I am grateful for:

WHAT HAPPENED TODAY

M| D| Y|

TIME: FEELING: INTENSITY (1–10):

SITUATION:

REACTION/STRATEGY:

ANXIETY LEVEL AFTER (1–10):

TIME: FEELING: INTENSITY (1–10):

SITUATION:

REACTION/STRATEGY:

ANXIETY LEVEL AFTER (1–10):

TIME: FEELING: INTENSITY (1–10):

SITUATION:

REACTION/STRATEGY:

ANXIETY LEVEL AFTER (1–10):

Self-Care

HOURS SLEPT:

NOURISHMENT (1-10):

WATER:

PHYSICAL ACTIVITY:

OTHER:

IMPACT ON MOOD (Y/N):

Today, I am grateful for:

WHAT HAPPENED TODAY

TIME: FEELING: INTENSITY (1–10):

SITUATION:

REACTION/STRATEGY:

                                                              ANXIETY LEVEL AFTER (1–10):

TIME: FEELING: INTENSITY (1–10):

SITUATION:

REACTION/STRATEGY:

                                                              ANXIETY LEVEL AFTER (1–10):

TIME: FEELING: INTENSITY (1–10):

SITUATION:

REACTION/STRATEGY:

                                                              ANXIETY LEVEL AFTER (1–10):

Self-Care

HOURS SLEPT:

NOURISHMENT (1-10):

WATER:

PHYSICAL ACTIVITY:

OTHER:

IMPACT ON MOOD (Y/N):

Today, I am grateful for:

WHAT HAPPENED TODAY

M| D| Y|

TIME: FEELING: INTENSITY (1–10):

SITUATION:

REACTION/STRATEGY:

ANXIETY LEVEL AFTER (1–10):

TIME: FEELING: INTENSITY (1–10):

SITUATION:

REACTION/STRATEGY:

ANXIETY LEVEL AFTER (1–10):

TIME: FEELING: INTENSITY (1–10):

SITUATION:

REACTION/STRATEGY:

ANXIETY LEVEL AFTER (1–10):

Self-Care

HOURS SLEPT:

NOURISHMENT (1-10):

WATER:

PHYSICAL ACTIVITY:

OTHER:

IMPACT ON MOOD (Y/N):

Today, I am grateful for:

| M| | D| | Y| |

WHAT HAPPENED TODAY

TIME: FEELING: INTENSITY (1–10):

SITUATION:

REACTION/STRATEGY:

ANXIETY LEVEL AFTER (1–10):

TIME: FEELING: INTENSITY (1–10):

SITUATION:

REACTION/STRATEGY:

ANXIETY LEVEL AFTER (1–10):

TIME: FEELING: INTENSITY (1–10):

SITUATION:

REACTION/STRATEGY:

ANXIETY LEVEL AFTER (1–10):

Self-Care

HOURS SLEPT:

NOURISHMENT (1-10):

WATER:

PHYSICAL ACTIVITY:

OTHER:

IMPACT ON MOOD (Y/N):

Today, I am grateful for:

WHAT HAPPENED TODAY

M| D| Y|

TIME: FEELING: INTENSITY (1-10):

SITUATION:

REACTION/STRATEGY:

ANXIETY LEVEL AFTER (1-10):

TIME: FEELING: INTENSITY (1-10):

SITUATION:

REACTION/STRATEGY:

ANXIETY LEVEL AFTER (1-10):

TIME: FEELING: INTENSITY (1-10):

SITUATION:

REACTION/STRATEGY:

ANXIETY LEVEL AFTER (1-10):

Self-Care   ## Today, I am grateful for:

HOURS SLEPT:

NOURISHMENT (1-10):

WATER:

PHYSICAL ACTIVITY:

OTHER:

IMPACT ON MOOD (Y/N):

| M| | D| | Y| |

WHAT HAPPENED TODAY

TIME: FEELING: INTENSITY (1–10):

SITUATION:

REACTION/STRATEGY:

ANXIETY LEVEL AFTER (1–10):

TIME: FEELING: INTENSITY (1–10):

SITUATION:

REACTION/STRATEGY:

ANXIETY LEVEL AFTER (1–10):

TIME: FEELING: INTENSITY (1–10):

SITUATION:

REACTION/STRATEGY:

ANXIETY LEVEL AFTER (1–10):

Self-Care

HOURS SLEPT:

NOURISHMENT (1-10):

WATER:

PHYSICAL ACTIVITY:

OTHER:

IMPACT ON MOOD (Y/N):

Today, I am grateful for:

WHAT HAPPENED TODAY

M| D| Y|

TIME: FEELING: INTENSITY (1–10):

SITUATION:

REACTION/STRATEGY:

ANXIETY LEVEL AFTER (1–10):

TIME: FEELING: INTENSITY (1–10):

SITUATION:

REACTION/STRATEGY:

ANXIETY LEVEL AFTER (1–10):

TIME: FEELING: INTENSITY (1–10):

SITUATION:

REACTION/STRATEGY:

ANXIETY LEVEL AFTER (1–10):

Self-Care

HOURS SLEPT:

NOURISHMENT (1-10):

WATER:

PHYSICAL ACTIVITY:

OTHER:

IMPACT ON MOOD (Y/N):

Today, I am grateful for:

WHAT HAPPENED TODAY

TIME: FEELING: INTENSITY (1–10):

SITUATION:

REACTION/STRATEGY:

ANXIETY LEVEL AFTER (1–10):

TIME: FEELING: INTENSITY (1–10):

SITUATION:

REACTION/STRATEGY:

ANXIETY LEVEL AFTER (1–10):

TIME: FEELING: INTENSITY (1–10):

SITUATION:

REACTION/STRATEGY:

ANXIETY LEVEL AFTER (1–10):

Self-Care

HOURS SLEPT:

NOURISHMENT (1-10):

WATER:

PHYSICAL ACTIVITY:

OTHER:

IMPACT ON MOOD (Y/N):

Today, I am grateful for:

WHAT HAPPENED TODAY

M| D| Y|

TIME: FEELING: INTENSITY (1–10):

SITUATION:

REACTION/STRATEGY:

ANXIETY LEVEL AFTER (1–10):

TIME: FEELING: INTENSITY (1–10):

SITUATION:

REACTION/STRATEGY:

ANXIETY LEVEL AFTER (1–10):

TIME: FEELING: INTENSITY (1–10):

SITUATION:

REACTION/STRATEGY:

ANXIETY LEVEL AFTER (1–10):

Self-Care

HOURS SLEPT:

NOURISHMENT (1-10):

WATER:

PHYSICAL ACTIVITY:

OTHER:

IMPACT ON MOOD (Y/N):

Today, I am grateful for:

| M| | D| | Y| |

WHAT HAPPENED TODAY

TIME: FEELING: INTENSITY (1-10):

SITUATION:

REACTION/STRATEGY:

ANXIETY LEVEL AFTER (1-10):

TIME: FEELING: INTENSITY (1-10):

SITUATION:

REACTION/STRATEGY:

ANXIETY LEVEL AFTER (1-10):

TIME: FEELING: INTENSITY (1-10):

SITUATION:

REACTION/STRATEGY:

ANXIETY LEVEL AFTER (1-10):

Self-Care

HOURS SLEPT:

NOURISHMENT (1-10):

WATER:

PHYSICAL ACTIVITY:

OTHER:

IMPACT ON MOOD (Y/N):

Today, I am grateful for:

WHAT HAPPENED TODAY

M| D| Y|

TIME: FEELING: INTENSITY (1-10):

SITUATION:

REACTION/STRATEGY:

ANXIETY LEVEL AFTER (1-10):

TIME: FEELING: INTENSITY (1-10):

SITUATION:

REACTION/STRATEGY:

ANXIETY LEVEL AFTER (1-10):

TIME: FEELING: INTENSITY (1-10):

SITUATION:

REACTION/STRATEGY:

ANXIETY LEVEL AFTER (1-10):

Self-Care

HOURS SLEPT:

NOURISHMENT (1-10):

WATER:

PHYSICAL ACTIVITY:

OTHER:

IMPACT ON MOOD (Y/N):

Today, I am grateful for:

WHAT HAPPENED TODAY

TIME: FEELING: INTENSITY (1–10):

SITUATION:

REACTION/STRATEGY:

ANXIETY LEVEL AFTER (1–10):

TIME: FEELING: INTENSITY (1–10):

SITUATION:

REACTION/STRATEGY:

ANXIETY LEVEL AFTER (1–10):

TIME: FEELING: INTENSITY (1–10):

SITUATION:

REACTION/STRATEGY:

ANXIETY LEVEL AFTER (1–10):

Self-Care

HOURS SLEPT:

NOURISHMENT (1-10):

WATER:

PHYSICAL ACTIVITY:

OTHER:

IMPACT ON MOOD (Y/N):

Today, I am grateful for:

WHAT HAPPENED TODAY

M| D| Y|

TIME: FEELING: INTENSITY (1–10):

SITUATION:

REACTION/STRATEGY:

ANXIETY LEVEL AFTER (1–10):

TIME: FEELING: INTENSITY (1–10):

SITUATION:

REACTION/STRATEGY:

ANXIETY LEVEL AFTER (1–10):

TIME: FEELING: INTENSITY (1–10):

SITUATION:

REACTION/STRATEGY:

ANXIETY LEVEL AFTER (1–10):

Self-Care

HOURS SLEPT:

NOURISHMENT (1-10):

WATER:

PHYSICAL ACTIVITY:

OTHER:

IMPACT ON MOOD (Y/N):

Today, I am grateful for:

| M| | D| | Y| |

WHAT HAPPENED TODAY

TIME: FEELING: INTENSITY (1–10):

SITUATION:

REACTION/STRATEGY:

ANXIETY LEVEL AFTER (1–10):

TIME: FEELING: INTENSITY (1–10):

SITUATION:

REACTION/STRATEGY:

ANXIETY LEVEL AFTER (1–10):

TIME: FEELING: INTENSITY (1–10):

SITUATION:

REACTION/STRATEGY:

ANXIETY LEVEL AFTER (1–10):

Self-Care

HOURS SLEPT:

NOURISHMENT (1-10):

WATER:

PHYSICAL ACTIVITY:

OTHER:

IMPACT ON MOOD (Y/N):

Today, I am grateful for:

WHAT HAPPENED TODAY

M| D| Y|

TIME: FEELING: INTENSITY (1–10):

SITUATION:

REACTION/STRATEGY:

ANXIETY LEVEL AFTER (1–10):

TIME: FEELING: INTENSITY (1–10):

SITUATION:

REACTION/STRATEGY:

ANXIETY LEVEL AFTER (1–10):

TIME: FEELING: INTENSITY (1–10):

SITUATION:

REACTION/STRATEGY:

ANXIETY LEVEL AFTER (1–10):

Self-Care

HOURS SLEPT:

NOURISHMENT (1-10):

WATER:

PHYSICAL ACTIVITY:

OTHER:

IMPACT ON MOOD (Y/N):

Today, I am grateful for:

WHAT HAPPENED TODAY

TIME: _____ FEELING: _____ INTENSITY (1–10): _____

SITUATION: _____

REACTION/STRATEGY: _____

ANXIETY LEVEL AFTER (1–10): _____

TIME: _____ FEELING: _____ INTENSITY (1–10): _____

SITUATION: _____

REACTION/STRATEGY: _____

ANXIETY LEVEL AFTER (1–10): _____

TIME: _____ FEELING: _____ INTENSITY (1–10): _____

SITUATION: _____

REACTION/STRATEGY: _____

ANXIETY LEVEL AFTER (1–10): _____

Self-Care

HOURS SLEPT: _____

NOURISHMENT (1-10): _____

WATER: _____

PHYSICAL ACTIVITY: _____

OTHER: _____

IMPACT ON MOOD (Y/N): _____

Today, I am grateful for:

WHAT HAPPENED TODAY

M| D| Y|

TIME: FEELING: INTENSITY (1-10):

SITUATION:

REACTION/STRATEGY:

ANXIETY LEVEL AFTER (1-10):

TIME: FEELING: INTENSITY (1-10):

SITUATION:

REACTION/STRATEGY:

ANXIETY LEVEL AFTER (1-10):

TIME: FEELING: INTENSITY (1-10):

SITUATION:

REACTION/STRATEGY:

ANXIETY LEVEL AFTER (1-10):

Self-Care

HOURS SLEPT:

NOURISHMENT (1-10):

WATER:

PHYSICAL ACTIVITY:

OTHER:

IMPACT ON MOOD (Y/N):

Today, I am grateful for:

| M| | D| | Y| |

WHAT HAPPENED TODAY

TIME: FEELING: INTENSITY (1–10):

SITUATION:

REACTION/STRATEGY:

ANXIETY LEVEL AFTER (1–10):

TIME: FEELING: INTENSITY (1–10):

SITUATION:

REACTION/STRATEGY:

ANXIETY LEVEL AFTER (1–10):

TIME: FEELING: INTENSITY (1–10):

SITUATION:

REACTION/STRATEGY:

ANXIETY LEVEL AFTER (1–10):

Self-Care

HOURS SLEPT:

NOURISHMENT (1-10):

WATER:

PHYSICAL ACTIVITY:

OTHER:

IMPACT ON MOOD (Y/N):

Today, I am grateful for:

WHAT HAPPENED TODAY

M| D| Y|

TIME: .... FEELING: .... INTENSITY (1–10): ....

SITUATION: ....

....

REACTION/STRATEGY: ....

....

ANXIETY LEVEL AFTER (1–10): ....

TIME: .... FEELING: .... INTENSITY (1–10): ....

SITUATION: ....

....

REACTION/STRATEGY: ....

....

ANXIETY LEVEL AFTER (1–10): ....

TIME: .... FEELING: .... INTENSITY (1–10): ....

SITUATION: ....

....

REACTION/STRATEGY: ....

....

ANXIETY LEVEL AFTER (1–10): ....

Self-Care

HOURS SLEPT: ....

NOURISHMENT (1-10): ....

WATER: ....

PHYSICAL ACTIVITY: ....

OTHER: ....

IMPACT ON MOOD (Y/N): ....

Today, I am grateful for:

| M| | D| | Y| |

WHAT HAPPENED TODAY

TIME: FEELING: INTENSITY (1–10):

SITUATION:

REACTION/STRATEGY:

ANXIETY LEVEL AFTER (1–10):

TIME: FEELING: INTENSITY (1–10):

SITUATION:

REACTION/STRATEGY:

ANXIETY LEVEL AFTER (1–10):

TIME: FEELING: INTENSITY (1–10):

SITUATION:

REACTION/STRATEGY:

ANXIETY LEVEL AFTER (1–10):

Self-Care

HOURS SLEPT:

NOURISHMENT (1-10):

WATER:

PHYSICAL ACTIVITY:

OTHER:

IMPACT ON MOOD (Y/N):

Today, I am grateful for:

WHAT HAPPENED TODAY

M| D| Y|

TIME: FEELING: INTENSITY (1–10):

SITUATION:

REACTION/STRATEGY:

ANXIETY LEVEL AFTER (1–10):

TIME: FEELING: INTENSITY (1–10):

SITUATION:

REACTION/STRATEGY:

ANXIETY LEVEL AFTER (1–10):

TIME: FEELING: INTENSITY (1–10):

SITUATION:

REACTION/STRATEGY:

ANXIETY LEVEL AFTER (1–10):

Self-Care

HOURS SLEPT:

NOURISHMENT (1-10):

WATER:

PHYSICAL ACTIVITY:

OTHER:

IMPACT ON MOOD (Y/N):

Today, I am grateful for:

| M| | D| | Y| |

WHAT HAPPENED TODAY

TIME: FEELING: INTENSITY (1–10):

SITUATION:

REACTION/STRATEGY:

ANXIETY LEVEL AFTER (1–10):

TIME: FEELING: INTENSITY (1–10):

SITUATION:

REACTION/STRATEGY:

ANXIETY LEVEL AFTER (1–10):

TIME: FEELING: INTENSITY (1–10):

SITUATION:

REACTION/STRATEGY:

ANXIETY LEVEL AFTER (1–10):

Self-Care

HOURS SLEPT:

NOURISHMENT (1-10):

WATER:

PHYSICAL ACTIVITY:

OTHER:

IMPACT ON MOOD (Y/N):

Today, I am grateful for:

Average Anxiety Level

① — ② — ③ — ④ — ⑤ — ⑥ — ⑦ — ⑧ — ⑨ — ⑩

2 Most Common Feelings

....

↓   WHAT LED UP TO THE FEELING   ↓

....

↓   STRATEGIES THAT WORKED OR DIDN'T WORK   ↓

↑ ↓ ↔ ....   ↑ ↓ ↔ ....

↑ ↓ ↔ ....   ↑ ↓ ↔ ....

↑ ↓ ↔ ....   ↑ ↓ ↔ ....

Self-Care That Helped Overall Mental Health

↑ ↓ ↔ ....

↑ ↓ ↔ ....

↑ ↓ ↔ ....

For Next Month

I WANT TO FOCUS ON CHANGING ONE THING:
....

THIS IS HOW I'LL DO IT:
....

....

Other Notes and Observations

WHAT HAPPENED TODAY

M| D| Y|

TIME: FEELING: INTENSITY (1–10):

SITUATION:

REACTION/STRATEGY:

ANXIETY LEVEL AFTER (1–10):

TIME: FEELING: INTENSITY (1–10):

SITUATION:

REACTION/STRATEGY:

ANXIETY LEVEL AFTER (1–10):

TIME: FEELING: INTENSITY (1–10):

SITUATION:

REACTION/STRATEGY:

ANXIETY LEVEL AFTER (1–10):

Self-Care

HOURS SLEPT:

NOURISHMENT (1-10):

WATER:

PHYSICAL ACTIVITY:

OTHER:

IMPACT ON MOOD (Y/N):

Today, I am grateful for:

| M| | D| | Y| |

WHAT HAPPENED TODAY

TIME: FEELING: INTENSITY (1–10):

SITUATION:

REACTION/STRATEGY:

ANXIETY LEVEL AFTER (1–10):

TIME: FEELING: INTENSITY (1–10):

SITUATION:

REACTION/STRATEGY:

ANXIETY LEVEL AFTER (1–10):

TIME: FEELING: INTENSITY (1–10):

SITUATION:

REACTION/STRATEGY:

ANXIETY LEVEL AFTER (1–10):

Self-Care

HOURS SLEPT:

NOURISHMENT (1-10):

WATER:

PHYSICAL ACTIVITY:

OTHER:

IMPACT ON MOOD (Y/N):

Today, I am grateful for:

WHAT HAPPENED TODAY

M| D| Y|

TIME: FEELING: INTENSITY (1-10):

SITUATION:

REACTION/STRATEGY:

ANXIETY LEVEL AFTER (1-10):

TIME: FEELING: INTENSITY (1-10):

SITUATION:

REACTION/STRATEGY:

ANXIETY LEVEL AFTER (1-10):

TIME: FEELING: INTENSITY (1-10):

SITUATION:

REACTION/STRATEGY:

ANXIETY LEVEL AFTER (1-10):

Self-Care

HOURS SLEPT:

NOURISHMENT (1-10):

WATER:

PHYSICAL ACTIVITY:

OTHER:

IMPACT ON MOOD (Y/N):

Today, I am grateful for:

| M| | D| | Y| |

WHAT HAPPENED TODAY

TIME: FEELING: INTENSITY (1–10):

SITUATION:

REACTION/STRATEGY:

ANXIETY LEVEL AFTER (1–10):

TIME: FEELING: INTENSITY (1–10):

SITUATION:

REACTION/STRATEGY:

ANXIETY LEVEL AFTER (1–10):

TIME: FEELING: INTENSITY (1–10):

SITUATION:

REACTION/STRATEGY:

ANXIETY LEVEL AFTER (1–10):

Self-Care

HOURS SLEPT:

NOURISHMENT (1-10):

WATER:

PHYSICAL ACTIVITY:

OTHER:

IMPACT ON MOOD (Y/N):

Today, I am grateful for:

WHAT HAPPENED TODAY

M| D| Y|

TIME: FEELING: INTENSITY (1–10):

SITUATION:

REACTION/STRATEGY:

ANXIETY LEVEL AFTER (1–10):

TIME: FEELING: INTENSITY (1–10):

SITUATION:

REACTION/STRATEGY:

ANXIETY LEVEL AFTER (1–10):

TIME: FEELING: INTENSITY (1–10):

SITUATION:

REACTION/STRATEGY:

ANXIETY LEVEL AFTER (1–10):

Self-Care

HOURS SLEPT:

NOURISHMENT (1-10):

WATER:

PHYSICAL ACTIVITY:

OTHER:

IMPACT ON MOOD (Y/N):

Today, I am grateful for:

| M| | D| | Y| |

WHAT HAPPENED TODAY

TIME: FEELING: INTENSITY (1–10):

SITUATION:

REACTION/STRATEGY:

ANXIETY LEVEL AFTER (1–10):

TIME: FEELING: INTENSITY (1–10):

SITUATION:

REACTION/STRATEGY:

ANXIETY LEVEL AFTER (1–10):

TIME: FEELING: INTENSITY (1–10):

SITUATION:

REACTION/STRATEGY:

ANXIETY LEVEL AFTER (1–10):

Self-Care

HOURS SLEPT:

NOURISHMENT (1-10):

WATER:

PHYSICAL ACTIVITY:

OTHER:

IMPACT ON MOOD (Y/N):

Today, I am grateful for:

WHAT HAPPENED TODAY

M| D| Y|

TIME: FEELING: INTENSITY (1–10):

SITUATION:

REACTION/STRATEGY:

ANXIETY LEVEL AFTER (1–10):

TIME: FEELING: INTENSITY (1–10):

SITUATION:

REACTION/STRATEGY:

ANXIETY LEVEL AFTER (1–10):

TIME: FEELING: INTENSITY (1–10):

SITUATION:

REACTION/STRATEGY:

ANXIETY LEVEL AFTER (1–10):

Self-Care

HOURS SLEPT:

NOURISHMENT (1-10):

WATER:

PHYSICAL ACTIVITY:

OTHER:

IMPACT ON MOOD (Y/N):

Today, I am grateful for:

| M| | D| | Y| | |

WHAT HAPPENED TODAY

TIME: FEELING: INTENSITY (1–10):

SITUATION:

REACTION/STRATEGY:

ANXIETY LEVEL AFTER (1–10):

TIME: FEELING: INTENSITY (1–10):

SITUATION:

REACTION/STRATEGY:

ANXIETY LEVEL AFTER (1–10):

TIME: FEELING: INTENSITY (1–10):

SITUATION:

REACTION/STRATEGY:

ANXIETY LEVEL AFTER (1–10):

Self-Care

HOURS SLEPT:

NOURISHMENT (1-10):

WATER:

PHYSICAL ACTIVITY:

OTHER:

IMPACT ON MOOD (Y/N):

Today, I am grateful for:

WHAT HAPPENED TODAY

M| D| Y|

TIME: FEELING: INTENSITY (1–10):

SITUATION:

REACTION/STRATEGY:

ANXIETY LEVEL AFTER (1–10):

TIME: FEELING: INTENSITY (1–10):

SITUATION:

REACTION/STRATEGY:

ANXIETY LEVEL AFTER (1–10):

TIME: FEELING: INTENSITY (1–10):

SITUATION:

REACTION/STRATEGY:

ANXIETY LEVEL AFTER (1–10):

Self-Care

HOURS SLEPT:

NOURISHMENT (1-10):

WATER:

PHYSICAL ACTIVITY:

OTHER:

IMPACT ON MOOD (Y/N):

Today, I am grateful for:

WHAT HAPPENED TODAY

TIME: FEELING: INTENSITY (1-10):

SITUATION:

REACTION/STRATEGY:

ANXIETY LEVEL AFTER (1-10):

TIME: FEELING: INTENSITY (1-10):

SITUATION:

REACTION/STRATEGY:

ANXIETY LEVEL AFTER (1-10):

TIME: FEELING: INTENSITY (1-10):

SITUATION:

REACTION/STRATEGY:

ANXIETY LEVEL AFTER (1-10):

Self-Care

HOURS SLEPT:

NOURISHMENT (1-10):

WATER:

PHYSICAL ACTIVITY:

OTHER:

IMPACT ON MOOD (Y/N):

Today, I am grateful for:

WHAT HAPPENED TODAY

M| D| Y|

TIME: FEELING: INTENSITY (1–10):

SITUATION:

REACTION/STRATEGY:

ANXIETY LEVEL AFTER (1–10):

TIME: FEELING: INTENSITY (1–10):

SITUATION:

REACTION/STRATEGY:

ANXIETY LEVEL AFTER (1–10):

TIME: FEELING: INTENSITY (1–10):

SITUATION:

REACTION/STRATEGY:

ANXIETY LEVEL AFTER (1–10):

Self-Care

HOURS SLEPT:

NOURISHMENT (1-10):

WATER:

PHYSICAL ACTIVITY:

OTHER:

IMPACT ON MOOD (Y/N):

Today, I am grateful for:

| M| | D| | Y| |

WHAT HAPPENED TODAY

TIME: FEELING: INTENSITY (1–10):

SITUATION:

REACTION/STRATEGY:

ANXIETY LEVEL AFTER (1–10):

TIME: FEELING: INTENSITY (1–10):

SITUATION:

REACTION/STRATEGY:

ANXIETY LEVEL AFTER (1–10):

TIME: FEELING: INTENSITY (1–10):

SITUATION:

REACTION/STRATEGY:

ANXIETY LEVEL AFTER (1–10):

Self-Care

HOURS SLEPT:

NOURISHMENT (1-10):

WATER:

PHYSICAL ACTIVITY:

OTHER:

IMPACT ON MOOD (Y/N):

Today, I am grateful for:

WHAT HAPPENED TODAY

M| D| Y|

TIME: FEELING: INTENSITY (1–10):

SITUATION:

REACTION/STRATEGY:

ANXIETY LEVEL AFTER (1–10):

TIME: FEELING: INTENSITY (1–10):

SITUATION:

REACTION/STRATEGY:

ANXIETY LEVEL AFTER (1–10):

TIME: FEELING: INTENSITY (1–10):

SITUATION:

REACTION/STRATEGY:

ANXIETY LEVEL AFTER (1–10):

Self-Care

HOURS SLEPT:

NOURISHMENT (1-10):

WATER:

PHYSICAL ACTIVITY:

OTHER:

IMPACT ON MOOD (Y/N):

Today, I am grateful for:

WHAT HAPPENED TODAY

TIME: FEELING: INTENSITY (1–10):

SITUATION:

REACTION/STRATEGY:

ANXIETY LEVEL AFTER (1–10):

TIME: FEELING: INTENSITY (1–10):

SITUATION:

REACTION/STRATEGY:

ANXIETY LEVEL AFTER (1–10):

TIME: FEELING: INTENSITY (1–10):

SITUATION:

REACTION/STRATEGY:

ANXIETY LEVEL AFTER (1–10):

Self-Care

HOURS SLEPT:

NOURISHMENT (1-10):

WATER:

PHYSICAL ACTIVITY:

OTHER:

IMPACT ON MOOD (Y/N):

Today, I am grateful for:

WHAT HAPPENED TODAY

M| D| Y|

TIME: FEELING: INTENSITY (1–10):

SITUATION:

REACTION/STRATEGY:

ANXIETY LEVEL AFTER (1–10):

TIME: FEELING: INTENSITY (1–10):

SITUATION:

REACTION/STRATEGY:

ANXIETY LEVEL AFTER (1–10):

TIME: FEELING: INTENSITY (1–10):

SITUATION:

REACTION/STRATEGY:

ANXIETY LEVEL AFTER (1–10):

Self-Care

HOURS SLEPT:

NOURISHMENT (1-10):

WATER:

PHYSICAL ACTIVITY:

OTHER:

IMPACT ON MOOD (Y/N):

Today, I am grateful for:

M| D| Y|

WHAT HAPPENED TODAY

TIME: FEELING: INTENSITY (1–10):

SITUATION:

REACTION/STRATEGY:

ANXIETY LEVEL AFTER (1–10):

TIME: FEELING: INTENSITY (1–10):

SITUATION:

REACTION/STRATEGY:

ANXIETY LEVEL AFTER (1–10):

TIME: FEELING: INTENSITY (1–10):

SITUATION:

REACTION/STRATEGY:

ANXIETY LEVEL AFTER (1–10):

Self-Care

HOURS SLEPT:

NOURISHMENT (1-10):

WATER:

PHYSICAL ACTIVITY:

OTHER:

IMPACT ON MOOD (Y/N):

Today, I am grateful for:

WHAT HAPPENED TODAY

M| D| Y|

TIME: FEELING: INTENSITY (1–10):

SITUATION:

REACTION/STRATEGY:

ANXIETY LEVEL AFTER (1–10):

TIME: FEELING: INTENSITY (1–10):

SITUATION:

REACTION/STRATEGY:

ANXIETY LEVEL AFTER (1–10):

TIME: FEELING: INTENSITY (1–10):

SITUATION:

REACTION/STRATEGY:

ANXIETY LEVEL AFTER (1–10):

Self-Care

HOURS SLEPT:

NOURISHMENT (1-10):

WATER:

PHYSICAL ACTIVITY:

OTHER:

IMPACT ON MOOD (Y/N):

Today, I am grateful for:

| M| | D| | Y| |

WHAT HAPPENED TODAY

TIME: FEELING: INTENSITY (1–10):

SITUATION:

REACTION/STRATEGY:

ANXIETY LEVEL AFTER (1–10):

TIME: FEELING: INTENSITY (1–10):

SITUATION:

REACTION/STRATEGY:

ANXIETY LEVEL AFTER (1–10):

TIME: FEELING: INTENSITY (1–10):

SITUATION:

REACTION/STRATEGY:

ANXIETY LEVEL AFTER (1–10):

Self-Care

HOURS SLEPT:

NOURISHMENT (1-10):

WATER:

PHYSICAL ACTIVITY:

OTHER:

IMPACT ON MOOD (Y/N):

Today, I am grateful for:

WHAT HAPPENED TODAY

M| D| Y|

TIME: FEELING: INTENSITY (1–10):

SITUATION:

REACTION/STRATEGY:

ANXIETY LEVEL AFTER (1–10):

TIME: FEELING: INTENSITY (1–10):

SITUATION:

REACTION/STRATEGY:

ANXIETY LEVEL AFTER (1–10):

TIME: FEELING: INTENSITY (1–10):

SITUATION:

REACTION/STRATEGY:

ANXIETY LEVEL AFTER (1–10):

Self-Care

HOURS SLEPT:

NOURISHMENT (1-10):

WATER:

PHYSICAL ACTIVITY:

OTHER:

IMPACT ON MOOD (Y/N):

Today, I am grateful for:

| M| | D| | Y| |

WHAT HAPPENED TODAY

TIME: .... FEELING: .... INTENSITY (1–10): ....

SITUATION: ....

....

REACTION/STRATEGY: ....

....

ANXIETY LEVEL AFTER (1–10): ....

TIME: .... FEELING: .... INTENSITY (1–10): ....

SITUATION: ....

....

REACTION/STRATEGY: ....

....

ANXIETY LEVEL AFTER (1–10): ....

TIME: .... FEELING: .... INTENSITY (1–10): ....

SITUATION: ....

....

REACTION/STRATEGY: ....

....

ANXIETY LEVEL AFTER (1–10): ....

Self-Care

HOURS SLEPT: ....

NOURISHMENT (1-10): ....

WATER: ....

PHYSICAL ACTIVITY: ....

....

OTHER: ....

IMPACT ON MOOD (Y/N): ....

Today, I am grateful for:

WHAT HAPPENED TODAY

M| D| Y|

TIME: FEELING: INTENSITY (1-10):

SITUATION:

REACTION/STRATEGY:

ANXIETY LEVEL AFTER (1-10):

TIME: FEELING: INTENSITY (1-10):

SITUATION:

REACTION/STRATEGY:

ANXIETY LEVEL AFTER (1-10):

TIME: FEELING: INTENSITY (1-10):

SITUATION:

REACTION/STRATEGY:

ANXIETY LEVEL AFTER (1-10):

Self-Care

HOURS SLEPT:

NOURISHMENT (1-10):

WATER:

PHYSICAL ACTIVITY:

OTHER:

IMPACT ON MOOD (Y/N):

Today, I am grateful for:

| M| | D| | Y| |

WHAT HAPPENED TODAY

TIME: FEELING: INTENSITY (1–10):

SITUATION:

REACTION/STRATEGY:

ANXIETY LEVEL AFTER (1–10):

TIME: FEELING: INTENSITY (1–10):

SITUATION:

REACTION/STRATEGY:

ANXIETY LEVEL AFTER (1–10):

TIME: FEELING: INTENSITY (1–10):

SITUATION:

REACTION/STRATEGY:

ANXIETY LEVEL AFTER (1–10):

Self-Care

HOURS SLEPT:

NOURISHMENT (1-10):

WATER:

PHYSICAL ACTIVITY:

OTHER:

IMPACT ON MOOD (Y/N):

Today, I am grateful for:

WHAT HAPPENED TODAY

M| D| Y|

TIME: FEELING: INTENSITY (1–10):

SITUATION:

REACTION/STRATEGY:

ANXIETY LEVEL AFTER (1–10):

TIME: FEELING: INTENSITY (1–10):

SITUATION:

REACTION/STRATEGY:

ANXIETY LEVEL AFTER (1–10):

TIME: FEELING: INTENSITY (1–10):

SITUATION:

REACTION/STRATEGY:

ANXIETY LEVEL AFTER (1–10):

Self-Care

HOURS SLEPT:

NOURISHMENT (1-10):

WATER:

PHYSICAL ACTIVITY:

OTHER:

IMPACT ON MOOD (Y/N):

Today, I am grateful for:

| M| | D| | Y| |

WHAT HAPPENED TODAY

TIME: FEELING: INTENSITY (1–10):

SITUATION:

REACTION/STRATEGY:

ANXIETY LEVEL AFTER (1–10):

TIME: FEELING: INTENSITY (1–10):

SITUATION:

REACTION/STRATEGY:

ANXIETY LEVEL AFTER (1–10):

TIME: FEELING: INTENSITY (1–10):

SITUATION:

REACTION/STRATEGY:

ANXIETY LEVEL AFTER (1–10):

Self-Care

HOURS SLEPT:

NOURISHMENT (1-10):

WATER:

PHYSICAL ACTIVITY:

OTHER:

IMPACT ON MOOD (Y/N):

Today, I am grateful for:

WHAT HAPPENED TODAY

M| D| Y|

TIME: FEELING: INTENSITY (1–10):

SITUATION:

REACTION/STRATEGY:

ANXIETY LEVEL AFTER (1–10):

TIME: FEELING: INTENSITY (1–10):

SITUATION:

REACTION/STRATEGY:

ANXIETY LEVEL AFTER (1–10):

TIME: FEELING: INTENSITY (1–10):

SITUATION:

REACTION/STRATEGY:

ANXIETY LEVEL AFTER (1–10):

Self-Care

HOURS SLEPT:

NOURISHMENT (1-10):

WATER:

PHYSICAL ACTIVITY:

OTHER:

IMPACT ON MOOD (Y/N):

Today, I am grateful for:

M| D| Y|

WHAT HAPPENED TODAY

TIME: FEELING: INTENSITY (1–10):

SITUATION:

REACTION/STRATEGY:

ANXIETY LEVEL AFTER (1–10):

TIME: FEELING: INTENSITY (1–10):

SITUATION:

REACTION/STRATEGY:

ANXIETY LEVEL AFTER (1–10):

TIME: FEELING: INTENSITY (1–10):

SITUATION:

REACTION/STRATEGY:

ANXIETY LEVEL AFTER (1–10):

Self-Care

HOURS SLEPT:

NOURISHMENT (1-10):

WATER:

PHYSICAL ACTIVITY:

OTHER:

IMPACT ON MOOD (Y/N):

Today, I am grateful for:

WHAT HAPPENED TODAY

M| D| Y|

TIME: FEELING: INTENSITY (1–10):

SITUATION:

REACTION/STRATEGY:

ANXIETY LEVEL AFTER (1–10):

TIME: FEELING: INTENSITY (1–10):

SITUATION:

REACTION/STRATEGY:

ANXIETY LEVEL AFTER (1–10):

TIME: FEELING: INTENSITY (1–10):

SITUATION:

REACTION/STRATEGY:

ANXIETY LEVEL AFTER (1–10):

Self-Care

HOURS SLEPT:

NOURISHMENT (1-10):

WATER:

PHYSICAL ACTIVITY:

OTHER:

IMPACT ON MOOD (Y/N):

Today, I am grateful for:

| M| | D| | Y| |

WHAT HAPPENED TODAY

TIME: FEELING: INTENSITY (1–10):

SITUATION:

REACTION/STRATEGY:

ANXIETY LEVEL AFTER (1–10):

TIME: FEELING: INTENSITY (1–10):

SITUATION:

REACTION/STRATEGY:

ANXIETY LEVEL AFTER (1–10):

TIME: FEELING: INTENSITY (1–10):

SITUATION:

REACTION/STRATEGY:

ANXIETY LEVEL AFTER (1–10):

Self-Care

HOURS SLEPT:

NOURISHMENT (1-10):

WATER:

PHYSICAL ACTIVITY:

OTHER:

IMPACT ON MOOD (Y/N):

Today, I am grateful for:

WHAT HAPPENED THIS MONTH   M| Y|

Average Anxiety Level

① ② ③ ④ ⑤ ⑥ ⑦ ⑧ ⑨ ⑩

2 Most Common Feelings

....

↓   WHAT LED UP TO THE FEELING   ↓

....

↓   STRATEGIES THAT WORKED OR DIDN'T WORK   ↓

↑ ↓ ↔   ↑ ↓ ↔

↑ ↓ ↔   ↑ ↓ ↔

↑ ↓ ↔   ↑ ↓ ↔

Self-Care That Helped Overall Mental Health

↑ ↓ ↔

↑ ↓ ↔

↑ ↓ ↔

For Next Month

I WANT TO FOCUS ON CHANGING ONE THING:

THIS IS HOW I'LL DO IT:

Other Notes and Observations

WHAT HAPPENED TODAY

M| D| Y|

TIME: FEELING: INTENSITY (1–10):

SITUATION:

REACTION/STRATEGY:

ANXIETY LEVEL AFTER (1–10):

TIME: FEELING: INTENSITY (1–10):

SITUATION:

REACTION/STRATEGY:

ANXIETY LEVEL AFTER (1–10):

TIME: FEELING: INTENSITY (1–10):

SITUATION:

REACTION/STRATEGY:

ANXIETY LEVEL AFTER (1–10):

Self-Care

HOURS SLEPT:

NOURISHMENT (1-10):

WATER:

PHYSICAL ACTIVITY:

OTHER:

IMPACT ON MOOD (Y/N):

Today, I am grateful for:

M|	D|	Y|

WHAT HAPPENED TODAY

TIME: FEELING: INTENSITY (1-10):

SITUATION:

REACTION/STRATEGY:

ANXIETY LEVEL AFTER (1-10):

TIME: FEELING: INTENSITY (1-10):

SITUATION:

REACTION/STRATEGY:

ANXIETY LEVEL AFTER (1-10):

TIME: FEELING: INTENSITY (1-10):

SITUATION:

REACTION/STRATEGY:

ANXIETY LEVEL AFTER (1-10):

Self-Care

HOURS SLEPT:

NOURISHMENT (1-10):

WATER:

PHYSICAL ACTIVITY:

OTHER:

IMPACT ON MOOD (Y/N):

Today, I am grateful for:

WHAT HAPPENED TODAY

M| D| Y|

TIME: FEELING: INTENSITY (1–10):

SITUATION:

REACTION/STRATEGY:

ANXIETY LEVEL AFTER (1–10):

TIME: FEELING: INTENSITY (1–10):

SITUATION:

REACTION/STRATEGY:

ANXIETY LEVEL AFTER (1–10):

TIME: FEELING: INTENSITY (1–10):

SITUATION:

REACTION/STRATEGY:

ANXIETY LEVEL AFTER (1–10):

Self-Care

HOURS SLEPT:

NOURISHMENT (1-10):

WATER:

PHYSICAL ACTIVITY:

OTHER:

IMPACT ON MOOD (Y/N):

Today, I am grateful for:

WHAT HAPPENED TODAY

TIME: FEELING: INTENSITY (1–10):

SITUATION:

REACTION/STRATEGY:

ANXIETY LEVEL AFTER (1–10):

TIME: FEELING: INTENSITY (1–10):

SITUATION:

REACTION/STRATEGY:

ANXIETY LEVEL AFTER (1–10):

TIME: FEELING: INTENSITY (1–10):

SITUATION:

REACTION/STRATEGY:

ANXIETY LEVEL AFTER (1–10):

Self-Care

HOURS SLEPT:

NOURISHMENT (1-10):

WATER:

PHYSICAL ACTIVITY:

OTHER:

IMPACT ON MOOD (Y/N):

Today, I am grateful for:

WHAT HAPPENED TODAY

M| D| Y|

TIME: FEELING: INTENSITY (1–10):

SITUATION:

REACTION/STRATEGY:

ANXIETY LEVEL AFTER (1–10):

TIME: FEELING: INTENSITY (1–10):

SITUATION:

REACTION/STRATEGY:

ANXIETY LEVEL AFTER (1–10):

TIME: FEELING: INTENSITY (1–10):

SITUATION:

REACTION/STRATEGY:

ANXIETY LEVEL AFTER (1–10):

Self-Care

HOURS SLEPT:

NOURISHMENT (1-10):

WATER:

PHYSICAL ACTIVITY:

OTHER:

IMPACT ON MOOD (Y/N):

Today, I am grateful for:

| M| | D| | Y| |

WHAT HAPPENED TODAY

TIME: FEELING: INTENSITY (1–10):

SITUATION:

REACTION/STRATEGY:

ANXIETY LEVEL AFTER (1–10):

TIME: FEELING: INTENSITY (1–10):

SITUATION:

REACTION/STRATEGY:

ANXIETY LEVEL AFTER (1–10):

TIME: FEELING: INTENSITY (1–10):

SITUATION:

REACTION/STRATEGY:

ANXIETY LEVEL AFTER (1–10):

Self-Care

HOURS SLEPT:

NOURISHMENT (1-10):

WATER:

PHYSICAL ACTIVITY:

OTHER:

IMPACT ON MOOD (Y/N):

Today, I am grateful for:

WHAT HAPPENED TODAY

M| D| Y|

TIME: FEELING: INTENSITY (1-10):

SITUATION:

REACTION/STRATEGY:

ANXIETY LEVEL AFTER (1-10):

TIME: FEELING: INTENSITY (1-10):

SITUATION:

REACTION/STRATEGY:

ANXIETY LEVEL AFTER (1-10):

TIME: FEELING: INTENSITY (1-10):

SITUATION:

REACTION/STRATEGY:

ANXIETY LEVEL AFTER (1-10):

Self-Care

HOURS SLEPT:

NOURISHMENT (1-10):

WATER:

PHYSICAL ACTIVITY:

OTHER:

IMPACT ON MOOD (Y/N):

Today, I am grateful for:

| M| | D| | Y| |

WHAT HAPPENED TODAY

TIME: FEELING: INTENSITY (1–10):

SITUATION:

REACTION/STRATEGY:

ANXIETY LEVEL AFTER (1–10):

TIME: FEELING: INTENSITY (1–10):

SITUATION:

REACTION/STRATEGY:

ANXIETY LEVEL AFTER (1–10):

TIME: FEELING: INTENSITY (1–10):

SITUATION:

REACTION/STRATEGY:

ANXIETY LEVEL AFTER (1–10):

Self-Care

HOURS SLEPT:

NOURISHMENT (1-10):

WATER:

PHYSICAL ACTIVITY:

OTHER:

IMPACT ON MOOD (Y/N):

Today, I am grateful for:

WHAT HAPPENED TODAY

M| D| Y|

TIME: FEELING: INTENSITY (1–10):

SITUATION:

REACTION/STRATEGY:

ANXIETY LEVEL AFTER (1–10):

TIME: FEELING: INTENSITY (1–10):

SITUATION:

REACTION/STRATEGY:

ANXIETY LEVEL AFTER (1–10):

TIME: FEELING: INTENSITY (1–10):

SITUATION:

REACTION/STRATEGY:

ANXIETY LEVEL AFTER (1–10):

Self-Care

HOURS SLEPT:

NOURISHMENT (1-10):

WATER:

PHYSICAL ACTIVITY:

OTHER:

IMPACT ON MOOD (Y/N):

Today, I am grateful for:

| M| | D| | Y| |

WHAT HAPPENED TODAY

TIME: FEELING: INTENSITY (1–10):

SITUATION:

REACTION/STRATEGY:

ANXIETY LEVEL AFTER (1–10):

TIME: FEELING: INTENSITY (1–10):

SITUATION:

REACTION/STRATEGY:

ANXIETY LEVEL AFTER (1–10):

TIME: FEELING: INTENSITY (1–10):

SITUATION:

REACTION/STRATEGY:

ANXIETY LEVEL AFTER (1–10):

Self-Care

HOURS SLEPT:

NOURISHMENT (1-10):

WATER:

PHYSICAL ACTIVITY:

OTHER:

IMPACT ON MOOD (Y/N):

Today, I am grateful for:

WHAT HAPPENED TODAY

M| D| Y|

TIME: FEELING: INTENSITY (1–10):

SITUATION:

REACTION/STRATEGY:

ANXIETY LEVEL AFTER (1–10):

TIME: FEELING: INTENSITY (1–10):

SITUATION:

REACTION/STRATEGY:

ANXIETY LEVEL AFTER (1–10):

TIME: FEELING: INTENSITY (1–10):

SITUATION:

REACTION/STRATEGY:

ANXIETY LEVEL AFTER (1–10):

Self-Care

HOURS SLEPT:

NOURISHMENT (1-10):

WATER:

PHYSICAL ACTIVITY:

OTHER:

IMPACT ON MOOD (Y/N):

Today, I am grateful for:

M| D| Y|

WHAT HAPPENED TODAY

TIME: FEELING: INTENSITY (1–10):

SITUATION:

REACTION/STRATEGY:

ANXIETY LEVEL AFTER (1–10):

TIME: FEELING: INTENSITY (1–10):

SITUATION:

REACTION/STRATEGY:

ANXIETY LEVEL AFTER (1–10):

TIME: FEELING: INTENSITY (1–10):

SITUATION:

REACTION/STRATEGY:

ANXIETY LEVEL AFTER (1–10):

Self-Care

HOURS SLEPT:

NOURISHMENT (1-10):

WATER:

PHYSICAL ACTIVITY:

OTHER:

IMPACT ON MOOD (Y/N):

Today, I am grateful for:

WHAT HAPPENED TODAY

M| D| Y|

TIME: FEELING: INTENSITY (1–10):

SITUATION:

REACTION/STRATEGY:

ANXIETY LEVEL AFTER (1–10):

TIME: FEELING: INTENSITY (1–10):

SITUATION:

REACTION/STRATEGY:

ANXIETY LEVEL AFTER (1–10):

TIME: FEELING: INTENSITY (1–10):

SITUATION:

REACTION/STRATEGY:

ANXIETY LEVEL AFTER (1–10):

Self-Care

HOURS SLEPT:

NOURISHMENT (1-10):

WATER:

PHYSICAL ACTIVITY:

OTHER:

IMPACT ON MOOD (Y/N):

Today, I am grateful for:

M| D| Y|

WHAT HAPPENED TODAY

TIME: FEELING: INTENSITY (1-10):

SITUATION:

REACTION/STRATEGY:

ANXIETY LEVEL AFTER (1-10):

TIME: FEELING: INTENSITY (1-10):

SITUATION:

REACTION/STRATEGY:

ANXIETY LEVEL AFTER (1-10):

TIME: FEELING: INTENSITY (1-10):

SITUATION:

REACTION/STRATEGY:

ANXIETY LEVEL AFTER (1-10):

Self-Care

HOURS SLEPT:

NOURISHMENT (1-10):

WATER:

PHYSICAL ACTIVITY:

OTHER:

IMPACT ON MOOD (Y/N):

Today, I am grateful for:

WHAT HAPPENED TODAY

M| D| Y|

TIME: FEELING: INTENSITY (1–10):

SITUATION:

REACTION/STRATEGY:

ANXIETY LEVEL AFTER (1–10):

TIME: FEELING: INTENSITY (1–10):

SITUATION:

REACTION/STRATEGY:

ANXIETY LEVEL AFTER (1–10):

TIME: FEELING: INTENSITY (1–10):

SITUATION:

REACTION/STRATEGY:

ANXIETY LEVEL AFTER (1–10):

Self-Care

HOURS SLEPT:

NOURISHMENT (1-10):

WATER:

PHYSICAL ACTIVITY:

OTHER:

IMPACT ON MOOD (Y/N):

Today, I am grateful for:

| M| | D| | Y| |

WHAT HAPPENED TODAY

TIME: FEELING: INTENSITY (1–10):

SITUATION:

REACTION/STRATEGY:

ANXIETY LEVEL AFTER (1–10):

TIME: FEELING: INTENSITY (1–10):

SITUATION:

REACTION/STRATEGY:

ANXIETY LEVEL AFTER (1–10):

TIME: FEELING: INTENSITY (1–10):

SITUATION:

REACTION/STRATEGY:

ANXIETY LEVEL AFTER (1–10):

Self-Care

HOURS SLEPT:

NOURISHMENT (1-10):

WATER:

PHYSICAL ACTIVITY:

OTHER:

IMPACT ON MOOD (Y/N):

Today, I am grateful for:

WHAT HAPPENED TODAY

M| D| Y|

TIME: FEELING: INTENSITY (1–10):

SITUATION:

REACTION/STRATEGY:

ANXIETY LEVEL AFTER (1–10):

TIME: FEELING: INTENSITY (1–10):

SITUATION:

REACTION/STRATEGY:

ANXIETY LEVEL AFTER (1–10):

TIME: FEELING: INTENSITY (1–10):

SITUATION:

REACTION/STRATEGY:

ANXIETY LEVEL AFTER (1–10):

Self-Care

HOURS SLEPT:

NOURISHMENT (1-10):

WATER:

PHYSICAL ACTIVITY:

OTHER:

IMPACT ON MOOD (Y/N):

Today, I am grateful for:

WHAT HAPPENED TODAY

TIME: FEELING: INTENSITY (1–10):

SITUATION:

REACTION/STRATEGY:

ANXIETY LEVEL AFTER (1–10):

TIME: FEELING: INTENSITY (1–10):

SITUATION:

REACTION/STRATEGY:

ANXIETY LEVEL AFTER (1–10):

TIME: FEELING: INTENSITY (1–10):

SITUATION:

REACTION/STRATEGY:

ANXIETY LEVEL AFTER (1–10):

Self-Care

HOURS SLEPT:

NOURISHMENT (1-10):

WATER:

PHYSICAL ACTIVITY:

OTHER:

IMPACT ON MOOD (Y/N):

Today, I am grateful for:

WHAT HAPPENED TODAY

M| D| Y|

TIME: FEELING: INTENSITY (1–10):

SITUATION:

REACTION/STRATEGY:

ANXIETY LEVEL AFTER (1–10):

TIME: FEELING: INTENSITY (1–10):

SITUATION:

REACTION/STRATEGY:

ANXIETY LEVEL AFTER (1–10):

TIME: FEELING: INTENSITY (1–10):

SITUATION:

REACTION/STRATEGY:

ANXIETY LEVEL AFTER (1–10):

Self-Care

HOURS SLEPT:

NOURISHMENT (1-10):

WATER:

PHYSICAL ACTIVITY:

OTHER:

IMPACT ON MOOD (Y/N):

Today, I am grateful for:

WHAT HAPPENED TODAY

TIME: FEELING: INTENSITY (1–10):

SITUATION:

REACTION/STRATEGY:

ANXIETY LEVEL AFTER (1–10):

TIME: FEELING: INTENSITY (1–10):

SITUATION:

REACTION/STRATEGY:

ANXIETY LEVEL AFTER (1–10):

TIME: FEELING: INTENSITY (1–10):

SITUATION:

REACTION/STRATEGY:

ANXIETY LEVEL AFTER (1–10):

Self-Care

HOURS SLEPT:

NOURISHMENT (1-10):

WATER:

PHYSICAL ACTIVITY:

OTHER:

IMPACT ON MOOD (Y/N):

Today, I am grateful for:

WHAT HAPPENED TODAY

| M| | D| | Y| |

TIME: FEELING: INTENSITY (1–10):

SITUATION:

REACTION/STRATEGY:

ANXIETY LEVEL AFTER (1–10):

TIME: FEELING: INTENSITY (1–10):

SITUATION:

REACTION/STRATEGY:

ANXIETY LEVEL AFTER (1–10):

TIME: FEELING: INTENSITY (1–10):

SITUATION:

REACTION/STRATEGY:

ANXIETY LEVEL AFTER (1–10):

Self-Care

HOURS SLEPT:

NOURISHMENT (1-10):

WATER:

PHYSICAL ACTIVITY:

OTHER:

IMPACT ON MOOD (Y/N):

Today, I am grateful for:

M|	D|	Y|

WHAT HAPPENED TODAY

TIME: FEELING: INTENSITY (1–10):

SITUATION:

REACTION/STRATEGY:

ANXIETY LEVEL AFTER (1–10):

TIME: FEELING: INTENSITY (1–10):

SITUATION:

REACTION/STRATEGY:

ANXIETY LEVEL AFTER (1–10):

TIME: FEELING: INTENSITY (1–10):

SITUATION:

REACTION/STRATEGY:

ANXIETY LEVEL AFTER (1–10):

Self-Care

HOURS SLEPT:

NOURISHMENT (1-10):

WATER:

PHYSICAL ACTIVITY:

OTHER:

IMPACT ON MOOD (Y/N):

Today, I am grateful for:

WHAT HAPPENED TODAY

M| D| Y|

TIME: FEELING: INTENSITY (1–10):

SITUATION:

REACTION/STRATEGY:

ANXIETY LEVEL AFTER (1–10):

TIME: FEELING: INTENSITY (1–10):

SITUATION:

REACTION/STRATEGY:

ANXIETY LEVEL AFTER (1–10):

TIME: FEELING: INTENSITY (1–10):

SITUATION:

REACTION/STRATEGY:

ANXIETY LEVEL AFTER (1–10):

Self-Care

HOURS SLEPT:

NOURISHMENT (1-10):

WATER:

PHYSICAL ACTIVITY:

OTHER:

IMPACT ON MOOD (Y/N):

Today, I am grateful for:

| M| D| Y| |

WHAT HAPPENED TODAY

TIME: FEELING: INTENSITY (1–10):

SITUATION:

REACTION/STRATEGY:

ANXIETY LEVEL AFTER (1–10):

TIME: FEELING: INTENSITY (1–10):

SITUATION:

REACTION/STRATEGY:

ANXIETY LEVEL AFTER (1–10):

TIME: FEELING: INTENSITY (1–10):

SITUATION:

REACTION/STRATEGY:

ANXIETY LEVEL AFTER (1–10):

Self-Care

HOURS SLEPT:

NOURISHMENT (1-10):

WATER:

PHYSICAL ACTIVITY:

OTHER:

IMPACT ON MOOD (Y/N):

Today, I am grateful for:

WHAT HAPPENED TODAY

M| D| Y|

TIME: FEELING: INTENSITY (1–10):

SITUATION:

REACTION/STRATEGY:

ANXIETY LEVEL AFTER (1–10):

TIME: FEELING: INTENSITY (1–10):

SITUATION:

REACTION/STRATEGY:

ANXIETY LEVEL AFTER (1–10):

TIME: FEELING: INTENSITY (1–10):

SITUATION:

REACTION/STRATEGY:

ANXIETY LEVEL AFTER (1–10):

Self-Care

HOURS SLEPT:

NOURISHMENT (1-10):

WATER:

PHYSICAL ACTIVITY:

OTHER:

IMPACT ON MOOD (Y/N):

Today, I am grateful for:

WHAT HAPPENED TODAY

TIME: FEELING: INTENSITY (1–10):

SITUATION:

REACTION/STRATEGY:

ANXIETY LEVEL AFTER (1–10):

TIME: FEELING: INTENSITY (1–10):

SITUATION:

REACTION/STRATEGY:

ANXIETY LEVEL AFTER (1–10):

TIME: FEELING: INTENSITY (1–10):

SITUATION:

REACTION/STRATEGY:

ANXIETY LEVEL AFTER (1–10):

Self-Care

HOURS SLEPT:

NOURISHMENT (1-10):

WATER:

PHYSICAL ACTIVITY:

OTHER:

IMPACT ON MOOD (Y/N):

Today, I am grateful for:

WHAT HAPPENED TODAY

M| D| Y|

TIME: FEELING: INTENSITY (1–10):

SITUATION:

REACTION/STRATEGY:

ANXIETY LEVEL AFTER (1–10):

TIME: FEELING: INTENSITY (1–10):

SITUATION:

REACTION/STRATEGY:

ANXIETY LEVEL AFTER (1–10):

TIME: FEELING: INTENSITY (1–10):

SITUATION:

REACTION/STRATEGY:

ANXIETY LEVEL AFTER (1–10):

Self-Care

HOURS SLEPT:

NOURISHMENT (1-10):

WATER:

PHYSICAL ACTIVITY:

OTHER:

IMPACT ON MOOD (Y/N):

Today, I am grateful for:

M| D| Y|

WHAT HAPPENED TODAY

TIME: FEELING: INTENSITY (1–10):

SITUATION:

REACTION/STRATEGY:

ANXIETY LEVEL AFTER (1–10):

TIME: FEELING: INTENSITY (1–10):

SITUATION:

REACTION/STRATEGY:

ANXIETY LEVEL AFTER (1–10):

TIME: FEELING: INTENSITY (1–10):

SITUATION:

REACTION/STRATEGY:

ANXIETY LEVEL AFTER (1–10):

Self-Care

HOURS SLEPT:

NOURISHMENT (1-10):

WATER:

PHYSICAL ACTIVITY:

OTHER:

IMPACT ON MOOD (Y/N):

Today, I am grateful for:

WHAT HAPPENED THIS MONTH

M| Y|

Average Anxiety Level

①   ②   ③   ④   ⑤   ⑥   ⑦   ⑧   ⑨   ⑩

2 Most Common Feelings

↓   WHAT LED UP TO THE FEELING   ↓

↓   STRATEGIES THAT WORKED OR DIDN'T WORK   ↓

↑   ↓   ↔   ↑   ↓   ↔

↑   ↓   ↔   ↑   ↓   ↔

↑   ↓   ↔   ↑   ↓   ↔

Self-Care That Helped Overall Mental Health

↑   ↓   ↔

↑   ↓   ↔

↑   ↓   ↔

For Next Month

I WANT TO FOCUS ON CHANGING ONE THING:

THIS IS HOW I'LL DO IT:

Other Notes and Observations

WHAT HAPPENED TODAY

| M| | D| | Y| |

TIME: FEELING: INTENSITY (1–10):

SITUATION:

REACTION/STRATEGY:

ANXIETY LEVEL AFTER (1–10):

TIME: FEELING: INTENSITY (1–10):

SITUATION:

REACTION/STRATEGY:

ANXIETY LEVEL AFTER (1–10):

TIME: FEELING: INTENSITY (1–10):

SITUATION:

REACTION/STRATEGY:

ANXIETY LEVEL AFTER (1–10):

Self-Care

HOURS SLEPT:

NOURISHMENT (1-10):

WATER:

PHYSICAL ACTIVITY:

OTHER:

IMPACT ON MOOD (Y/N):

Today, I am grateful for:

| M| | D| | Y| |

WHAT HAPPENED TODAY

TIME: FEELING: INTENSITY (1–10):

SITUATION:

REACTION/STRATEGY:

ANXIETY LEVEL AFTER (1–10):

TIME: FEELING: INTENSITY (1–10):

SITUATION:

REACTION/STRATEGY:

ANXIETY LEVEL AFTER (1–10):

TIME: FEELING: INTENSITY (1–10):

SITUATION:

REACTION/STRATEGY:

ANXIETY LEVEL AFTER (1–10):

Self-Care

HOURS SLEPT:

NOURISHMENT (1-10):

WATER:

PHYSICAL ACTIVITY:

OTHER:

IMPACT ON MOOD (Y/N):

Today, I am grateful for:

WHAT HAPPENED TODAY

M| D| Y|

TIME: FEELING: INTENSITY (1–10):

SITUATION:

REACTION/STRATEGY:

ANXIETY LEVEL AFTER (1–10):

TIME: FEELING: INTENSITY (1–10):

SITUATION:

REACTION/STRATEGY:

ANXIETY LEVEL AFTER (1–10):

TIME: FEELING: INTENSITY (1–10):

SITUATION:

REACTION/STRATEGY:

ANXIETY LEVEL AFTER (1–10):

Self-Care

HOURS SLEPT:

NOURISHMENT (1-10):

WATER:

PHYSICAL ACTIVITY:

OTHER:

IMPACT ON MOOD (Y/N):

Today, I am grateful for:

WHAT HAPPENED TODAY

TIME: FEELING: INTENSITY (1–10):

SITUATION:

REACTION/STRATEGY:

ANXIETY LEVEL AFTER (1–10):

TIME: FEELING: INTENSITY (1–10):

SITUATION:

REACTION/STRATEGY:

ANXIETY LEVEL AFTER (1–10):

TIME: FEELING: INTENSITY (1–10):

SITUATION:

REACTION/STRATEGY:

ANXIETY LEVEL AFTER (1–10):

Self-Care

HOURS SLEPT:

NOURISHMENT (1-10):

WATER:

PHYSICAL ACTIVITY:

OTHER:

IMPACT ON MOOD (Y/N):

Today, I am grateful for:

WHAT HAPPENED TODAY

M|　　　　D|　　　　Y|

TIME:　　　　　FEELING:　　　　　　　　　　INTENSITY (1–10):

SITUATION:

REACTION/STRATEGY:

ANXIETY LEVEL AFTER (1–10):

TIME:　　　　　FEELING:　　　　　　　　　　INTENSITY (1–10):

SITUATION:

REACTION/STRATEGY:

ANXIETY LEVEL AFTER (1–10):

TIME:　　　　　FEELING:　　　　　　　　　　INTENSITY (1–10):

SITUATION:

REACTION/STRATEGY:

ANXIETY LEVEL AFTER (1–10):

Self-Care

HOURS SLEPT:

NOURISHMENT (1-10):

WATER:

PHYSICAL ACTIVITY:

OTHER:

IMPACT ON MOOD (Y/N):

Today, I am grateful for:

M| D| Y|

WHAT HAPPENED TODAY

TIME: FEELING: INTENSITY (1–10):

SITUATION:

REACTION/STRATEGY:

ANXIETY LEVEL AFTER (1–10):

TIME: FEELING: INTENSITY (1–10):

SITUATION:

REACTION/STRATEGY:

ANXIETY LEVEL AFTER (1–10):

TIME: FEELING: INTENSITY (1–10):

SITUATION:

REACTION/STRATEGY:

ANXIETY LEVEL AFTER (1–10):

Self-Care

HOURS SLEPT:

NOURISHMENT (1-10):

WATER:

PHYSICAL ACTIVITY:

OTHER:

IMPACT ON MOOD (Y/N):

Today, I am grateful for:

WHAT HAPPENED TODAY

M| D| Y|

TIME: FEELING: INTENSITY (1–10):

SITUATION:

REACTION/STRATEGY:

ANXIETY LEVEL AFTER (1–10):

TIME: FEELING: INTENSITY (1–10):

SITUATION:

REACTION/STRATEGY:

ANXIETY LEVEL AFTER (1–10):

TIME: FEELING: INTENSITY (1–10):

SITUATION:

REACTION/STRATEGY:

ANXIETY LEVEL AFTER (1–10):

Self-Care

HOURS SLEPT:

NOURISHMENT (1-10):

WATER:

PHYSICAL ACTIVITY:

OTHER:

IMPACT ON MOOD (Y/N):

Today, I am grateful for:

| M| | D| | Y| |

WHAT HAPPENED TODAY

TIME: FEELING: INTENSITY (1–10):

SITUATION:

REACTION/STRATEGY:

ANXIETY LEVEL AFTER (1–10):

TIME: FEELING: INTENSITY (1–10):

SITUATION:

REACTION/STRATEGY:

ANXIETY LEVEL AFTER (1–10):

TIME: FEELING: INTENSITY (1–10):

SITUATION:

REACTION/STRATEGY:

ANXIETY LEVEL AFTER (1–10):

Self-Care

HOURS SLEPT:

NOURISHMENT (1-10):

WATER:

PHYSICAL ACTIVITY:

OTHER:

IMPACT ON MOOD (Y/N):

Today, I am grateful for:

WHAT HAPPENED TODAY

M| D| Y|

TIME: FEELING: INTENSITY (1–10):

SITUATION:

REACTION/STRATEGY:

ANXIETY LEVEL AFTER (1–10):

TIME: FEELING: INTENSITY (1–10):

SITUATION:

REACTION/STRATEGY:

ANXIETY LEVEL AFTER (1–10):

TIME: FEELING: INTENSITY (1–10):

SITUATION:

REACTION/STRATEGY:

ANXIETY LEVEL AFTER (1–10):

Self-Care

HOURS SLEPT:

NOURISHMENT (1-10):

WATER:

PHYSICAL ACTIVITY:

OTHER:

IMPACT ON MOOD (Y/N):

Today, I am grateful for:

WHAT HAPPENED TODAY

TIME: FEELING: INTENSITY (1–10):

SITUATION:

REACTION/STRATEGY:

ANXIETY LEVEL AFTER (1–10):

TIME: FEELING: INTENSITY (1–10):

SITUATION:

REACTION/STRATEGY:

ANXIETY LEVEL AFTER (1–10):

TIME: FEELING: INTENSITY (1–10):

SITUATION:

REACTION/STRATEGY:

ANXIETY LEVEL AFTER (1–10):

Self-Care

HOURS SLEPT:

NOURISHMENT (1-10):

WATER:

PHYSICAL ACTIVITY:

OTHER:

IMPACT ON MOOD (Y/N):

Today, I am grateful for:

WHAT HAPPENED TODAY

M| D| Y|

TIME: FEELING: INTENSITY (1–10):

SITUATION:

REACTION/STRATEGY:

ANXIETY LEVEL AFTER (1–10):

TIME: FEELING: INTENSITY (1–10):

SITUATION:

REACTION/STRATEGY:

ANXIETY LEVEL AFTER (1–10):

TIME: FEELING: INTENSITY (1–10):

SITUATION:

REACTION/STRATEGY:

ANXIETY LEVEL AFTER (1–10):

Self-Care

HOURS SLEPT:

NOURISHMENT (1-10):

WATER:

PHYSICAL ACTIVITY:

OTHER:

IMPACT ON MOOD (Y/N):

Today, I am grateful for:

| M| | D| | Y| |

WHAT HAPPENED TODAY

TIME: FEELING: INTENSITY (1–10):

SITUATION:

REACTION/STRATEGY:

ANXIETY LEVEL AFTER (1–10):

TIME: FEELING: INTENSITY (1–10):

SITUATION:

REACTION/STRATEGY:

ANXIETY LEVEL AFTER (1–10):

TIME: FEELING: INTENSITY (1–10):

SITUATION:

REACTION/STRATEGY:

ANXIETY LEVEL AFTER (1–10):

Self-Care

HOURS SLEPT:

NOURISHMENT (1-10):

WATER:

PHYSICAL ACTIVITY:

OTHER:

IMPACT ON MOOD (Y/N):

Today, I am grateful for:

WHAT HAPPENED TODAY

M| D| Y|

TIME: FEELING: INTENSITY (1–10):

SITUATION:

REACTION/STRATEGY:

ANXIETY LEVEL AFTER (1–10):

TIME: FEELING: INTENSITY (1–10):

SITUATION:

REACTION/STRATEGY:

ANXIETY LEVEL AFTER (1–10):

TIME: FEELING: INTENSITY (1–10):

SITUATION:

REACTION/STRATEGY:

ANXIETY LEVEL AFTER (1–10):

Self-Care

HOURS SLEPT:

NOURISHMENT (1-10):

WATER:

PHYSICAL ACTIVITY:

OTHER:

IMPACT ON MOOD (Y/N):

Today, I am grateful for:

| M| | D| | Y| |

WHAT HAPPENED TODAY

TIME: FEELING: INTENSITY (1–10):

SITUATION:

REACTION/STRATEGY:

ANXIETY LEVEL AFTER (1–10):

TIME: FEELING: INTENSITY (1–10):

SITUATION:

REACTION/STRATEGY:

ANXIETY LEVEL AFTER (1–10):

TIME: FEELING: INTENSITY (1–10):

SITUATION:

REACTION/STRATEGY:

ANXIETY LEVEL AFTER (1–10):

Self-Care

HOURS SLEPT:

NOURISHMENT (1-10):

WATER:

PHYSICAL ACTIVITY:

OTHER:

IMPACT ON MOOD (Y/N):

Today, I am grateful for:

WHAT HAPPENED TODAY

M| D| Y|

TIME: FEELING: INTENSITY (1–10):

SITUATION:

REACTION/STRATEGY:

ANXIETY LEVEL AFTER (1–10):

TIME: FEELING: INTENSITY (1–10):

SITUATION:

REACTION/STRATEGY:

ANXIETY LEVEL AFTER (1–10):

TIME: FEELING: INTENSITY (1–10):

SITUATION:

REACTION/STRATEGY:

ANXIETY LEVEL AFTER (1–10):

Self-Care

HOURS SLEPT:

NOURISHMENT (1-10):

WATER:

PHYSICAL ACTIVITY:

OTHER:

IMPACT ON MOOD (Y/N):

Today, I am grateful for:

| M| | D| | Y| |

WHAT HAPPENED TODAY

TIME: FEELING: INTENSITY (1–10):

SITUATION:

REACTION/STRATEGY:

ANXIETY LEVEL AFTER (1–10):

TIME: FEELING: INTENSITY (1–10):

SITUATION:

REACTION/STRATEGY:

ANXIETY LEVEL AFTER (1–10):

TIME: FEELING: INTENSITY (1–10):

SITUATION:

REACTION/STRATEGY:

ANXIETY LEVEL AFTER (1–10):

Self-Care

HOURS SLEPT:

NOURISHMENT (1-10):

WATER:

PHYSICAL ACTIVITY:

OTHER:

IMPACT ON MOOD (Y/N):

Today, I am grateful for:

WHAT HAPPENED TODAY

M| D| Y|

TIME: FEELING: INTENSITY (1–10):

SITUATION:

REACTION/STRATEGY:

ANXIETY LEVEL AFTER (1–10):

TIME: FEELING: INTENSITY (1–10):

SITUATION:

REACTION/STRATEGY:

ANXIETY LEVEL AFTER (1–10):

TIME: FEELING: INTENSITY (1–10):

SITUATION:

REACTION/STRATEGY:

ANXIETY LEVEL AFTER (1–10):

Self-Care

HOURS SLEPT:

NOURISHMENT (1-10):

WATER:

PHYSICAL ACTIVITY:

OTHER:

IMPACT ON MOOD (Y/N):

Today, I am grateful for:

| M| | D| | Y| |

WHAT HAPPENED TODAY

TIME: FEELING: INTENSITY (1–10):

SITUATION:

REACTION/STRATEGY:

ANXIETY LEVEL AFTER (1–10):

TIME: FEELING: INTENSITY (1–10):

SITUATION:

REACTION/STRATEGY:

ANXIETY LEVEL AFTER (1–10):

TIME: FEELING: INTENSITY (1–10):

SITUATION:

REACTION/STRATEGY:

ANXIETY LEVEL AFTER (1–10):

Self-Care

HOURS SLEPT:

NOURISHMENT (1-10):

WATER:

PHYSICAL ACTIVITY:

OTHER:

IMPACT ON MOOD (Y/N):

Today, I am grateful for:

WHAT HAPPENED TODAY

M| D| Y|

TIME: FEELING: INTENSITY (1–10):

SITUATION:

REACTION/STRATEGY:

ANXIETY LEVEL AFTER (1–10):

TIME: FEELING: INTENSITY (1–10):

SITUATION:

REACTION/STRATEGY:

ANXIETY LEVEL AFTER (1–10):

TIME: FEELING: INTENSITY (1–10):

SITUATION:

REACTION/STRATEGY:

ANXIETY LEVEL AFTER (1–10):

Self-Care

HOURS SLEPT:

NOURISHMENT (1-10):

WATER:

PHYSICAL ACTIVITY:

OTHER:

IMPACT ON MOOD (Y/N):

Today, I am grateful for:

WHAT HAPPENED TODAY

TIME: FEELING: INTENSITY (1–10):

SITUATION:

REACTION/STRATEGY:

ANXIETY LEVEL AFTER (1–10):

TIME: FEELING: INTENSITY (1–10):

SITUATION:

REACTION/STRATEGY:

ANXIETY LEVEL AFTER (1–10):

TIME: FEELING: INTENSITY (1–10):

SITUATION:

REACTION/STRATEGY:

ANXIETY LEVEL AFTER (1–10):

Self-Care

HOURS SLEPT:

NOURISHMENT (1-10):

WATER:

PHYSICAL ACTIVITY:

OTHER:

IMPACT ON MOOD (Y/N):

Today, I am grateful for:

WHAT HAPPENED TODAY

M| D| Y| .

TIME: FEELING: INTENSITY (1–10):

SITUATION:

REACTION/STRATEGY:

ANXIETY LEVEL AFTER (1–10):

TIME: FEELING: INTENSITY (1–10):

SITUATION:

REACTION/STRATEGY:

ANXIETY LEVEL AFTER (1–10):

TIME: FEELING: INTENSITY (1–10):

SITUATION:

REACTION/STRATEGY:

ANXIETY LEVEL AFTER (1–10):

Self-Care

HOURS SLEPT:

NOURISHMENT (1-10):

WATER:

PHYSICAL ACTIVITY:

OTHER:

IMPACT ON MOOD (Y/N):

Today, I am grateful for:

| M| | D| | Y| |

WHAT HAPPENED TODAY

TIME: FEELING: INTENSITY (1–10):

SITUATION:

REACTION/STRATEGY:

ANXIETY LEVEL AFTER (1–10):

TIME: FEELING: INTENSITY (1–10):

SITUATION:

REACTION/STRATEGY:

ANXIETY LEVEL AFTER (1–10):

TIME: FEELING: INTENSITY (1–10):

SITUATION:

REACTION/STRATEGY:

ANXIETY LEVEL AFTER (1–10):

Self-Care

HOURS SLEPT:

NOURISHMENT (1-10):

WATER:

PHYSICAL ACTIVITY:

OTHER:

IMPACT ON MOOD (Y/N):

Today, I am grateful for:

WHAT HAPPENED TODAY

M| D| Y|

TIME: FEELING: INTENSITY (1–10):

SITUATION:

REACTION/STRATEGY:

ANXIETY LEVEL AFTER (1–10):

TIME: FEELING: INTENSITY (1–10):

SITUATION:

REACTION/STRATEGY:

ANXIETY LEVEL AFTER (1–10):

TIME: FEELING: INTENSITY (1–10):

SITUATION:

REACTION/STRATEGY:

ANXIETY LEVEL AFTER (1–10):

Self-Care

HOURS SLEPT:

NOURISHMENT (1-10):

WATER:

PHYSICAL ACTIVITY:

OTHER:

IMPACT ON MOOD (Y/N):

Today, I am grateful for:

| M| | D| | Y| |

WHAT HAPPENED TODAY

TIME: FEELING: INTENSITY (1–10):

SITUATION:

REACTION/STRATEGY:

ANXIETY LEVEL AFTER (1–10):

TIME: FEELING: INTENSITY (1–10):

SITUATION:

REACTION/STRATEGY:

ANXIETY LEVEL AFTER (1–10):

TIME: FEELING: INTENSITY (1–10):

SITUATION:

REACTION/STRATEGY:

ANXIETY LEVEL AFTER (1–10):

Self-Care

HOURS SLEPT:

NOURISHMENT (1-10):

WATER:

PHYSICAL ACTIVITY:

OTHER:

IMPACT ON MOOD (Y/N):

Today, I am grateful for:

WHAT HAPPENED TODAY

M| D| Y|

TIME: FEELING: INTENSITY (1-10):

SITUATION:

REACTION/STRATEGY:

ANXIETY LEVEL AFTER (1-10):

TIME: FEELING: INTENSITY (1-10):

SITUATION:

REACTION/STRATEGY:

ANXIETY LEVEL AFTER (1-10):

TIME: FEELING: INTENSITY (1-10):

SITUATION:

REACTION/STRATEGY:

ANXIETY LEVEL AFTER (1-10):

Self-Care

HOURS SLEPT:

NOURISHMENT (1-10):

WATER:

PHYSICAL ACTIVITY:

OTHER:

IMPACT ON MOOD (Y/N):

Today, I am grateful for:

| M| | D| | Y| |

WHAT HAPPENED TODAY

TIME: FEELING: INTENSITY (1–10):

SITUATION:

REACTION/STRATEGY:

ANXIETY LEVEL AFTER (1–10):

TIME: FEELING: INTENSITY (1–10):

SITUATION:

REACTION/STRATEGY:

ANXIETY LEVEL AFTER (1–10):

TIME: FEELING: INTENSITY (1–10):

SITUATION:

REACTION/STRATEGY:

ANXIETY LEVEL AFTER (1–10):

Self-Care

HOURS SLEPT:

NOURISHMENT (1-10):

WATER:

PHYSICAL ACTIVITY:

OTHER:

IMPACT ON MOOD (Y/N):

Today, I am grateful for:

WHAT HAPPENED TODAY

M| D| Y|

TIME: FEELING: INTENSITY (1–10):

SITUATION:

REACTION/STRATEGY:

ANXIETY LEVEL AFTER (1–10):

TIME: FEELING: INTENSITY (1–10):

SITUATION:

REACTION/STRATEGY:

ANXIETY LEVEL AFTER (1–10):

TIME: FEELING: INTENSITY (1–10):

SITUATION:

REACTION/STRATEGY:

ANXIETY LEVEL AFTER (1–10):

Self-Care

HOURS SLEPT:

NOURISHMENT (1-10):

WATER:

PHYSICAL ACTIVITY:

OTHER:

IMPACT ON MOOD (Y/N):

Today, I am grateful for:

M| D| Y|

TIME: FEELING: INTENSITY (1-10):

SITUATION:

REACTION/STRATEGY:

ANXIETY LEVEL AFTER (1-10):

TIME: FEELING: INTENSITY (1-10):

SITUATION:

REACTION/STRATEGY:

ANXIETY LEVEL AFTER (1-10):

TIME: FEELING: INTENSITY (1-10):

SITUATION:

REACTION/STRATEGY:

ANXIETY LEVEL AFTER (1-10):

Self-Care

HOURS SLEPT:

NOURISHMENT (1-10):

WATER:

PHYSICAL ACTIVITY:

OTHER:

IMPACT ON MOOD (Y/N):

Today, I am grateful for:

Average Anxiety Level

① ② ③ ④ ⑤ ⑥ ⑦ ⑧ ⑨ ⑩

2 Most Common Feelings

↓   WHAT LED UP TO THE FEELING   ↓

↓   STRATEGIES THAT WORKED OR DIDN'T WORK   ↓

↑ ↓ ↔   ↑ ↓ ↔

↑ ↓ ↔   ↑ ↓ ↔

↑ ↓ ↔   ↑ ↓ ↔

Self-Care That Helped Overall Mental Health

↑ ↓ ↔

↑ ↓ ↔

↑ ↓ ↔

For Next Month

I WANT TO FOCUS ON CHANGING ONE THING:

THIS IS HOW I'LL DO IT:

Other Notes and Observations

WHAT HAPPENED TODAY

M| D| Y|

TIME: FEELING: INTENSITY (1–10):

SITUATION:

REACTION/STRATEGY:

ANXIETY LEVEL AFTER (1–10):

TIME: FEELING: INTENSITY (1–10):

SITUATION:

REACTION/STRATEGY:

ANXIETY LEVEL AFTER (1–10):

TIME: FEELING: INTENSITY (1–10):

SITUATION:

REACTION/STRATEGY:

ANXIETY LEVEL AFTER (1–10):

Self-Care

HOURS SLEPT:

NOURISHMENT (1-10):

WATER:

PHYSICAL ACTIVITY:

OTHER:

IMPACT ON MOOD (Y/N):

Today, I am grateful for:

| M| | D| | Y| |

WHAT HAPPENED TODAY

TIME: FEELING: INTENSITY (1–10):

SITUATION:

REACTION/STRATEGY:

ANXIETY LEVEL AFTER (1–10):

TIME: FEELING: INTENSITY (1–10):

SITUATION:

REACTION/STRATEGY:

ANXIETY LEVEL AFTER (1–10):

TIME: FEELING: INTENSITY (1–10):

SITUATION:

REACTION/STRATEGY:

ANXIETY LEVEL AFTER (1–10):

Self-Care

HOURS SLEPT:

NOURISHMENT (1–10):

WATER:

PHYSICAL ACTIVITY:

OTHER:

IMPACT ON MOOD (Y/N):

Today, I am grateful for:

WHAT HAPPENED TODAY

M| D| Y|

TIME: FEELING: INTENSITY (1–10):

SITUATION:

REACTION/STRATEGY:

ANXIETY LEVEL AFTER (1–10):

TIME: FEELING: INTENSITY (1–10):

SITUATION:

REACTION/STRATEGY:

ANXIETY LEVEL AFTER (1–10):

TIME: FEELING: INTENSITY (1–10):

SITUATION:

REACTION/STRATEGY:

ANXIETY LEVEL AFTER (1–10):

Self-Care

HOURS SLEPT:

NOURISHMENT (1-10):

WATER:

PHYSICAL ACTIVITY:

OTHER:

IMPACT ON MOOD (Y/N):

Today, I am grateful for:

WHAT HAPPENED TODAY

TIME: FEELING: INTENSITY (1–10):

SITUATION:

REACTION/STRATEGY:

ANXIETY LEVEL AFTER (1–10):

TIME: FEELING: INTENSITY (1–10):

SITUATION:

REACTION/STRATEGY:

ANXIETY LEVEL AFTER (1–10):

TIME: FEELING: INTENSITY (1–10):

SITUATION:

REACTION/STRATEGY:

ANXIETY LEVEL AFTER (1–10):

Self-Care

HOURS SLEPT:

NOURISHMENT (1-10):

WATER:

PHYSICAL ACTIVITY:

OTHER:

IMPACT ON MOOD (Y/N):

Today, I am grateful for:

WHAT HAPPENED TODAY

M| D| Y|

TIME: FEELING: INTENSITY (1–10):

SITUATION:

REACTION/STRATEGY:

ANXIETY LEVEL AFTER (1–10):

TIME: FEELING: INTENSITY (1–10):

SITUATION:

REACTION/STRATEGY:

ANXIETY LEVEL AFTER (1–10):

TIME: FEELING: INTENSITY (1–10):

SITUATION:

REACTION/STRATEGY:

ANXIETY LEVEL AFTER (1–10):

Self-Care

HOURS SLEPT:

NOURISHMENT (1-10):

WATER:

PHYSICAL ACTIVITY:

OTHER:

IMPACT ON MOOD (Y/N):

Today, I am grateful for:

M| D| Y|

WHAT HAPPENED TODAY

TIME: FEELING: INTENSITY (1–10):

SITUATION:

REACTION/STRATEGY:

ANXIETY LEVEL AFTER (1–10):

TIME: FEELING: INTENSITY (1–10):

SITUATION:

REACTION/STRATEGY:

ANXIETY LEVEL AFTER (1–10):

TIME: FEELING: INTENSITY (1–10):

SITUATION:

REACTION/STRATEGY:

ANXIETY LEVEL AFTER (1–10):

Self-Care

HOURS SLEPT:

NOURISHMENT (1-10):

WATER:

PHYSICAL ACTIVITY:

OTHER:

IMPACT ON MOOD (Y/N):

Today, I am grateful for:

WHAT HAPPENED TODAY

M| D| Y|

TIME: FEELING: INTENSITY (1–10):

SITUATION:

REACTION/STRATEGY:

ANXIETY LEVEL AFTER (1–10):

TIME: FEELING: INTENSITY (1–10):

SITUATION:

REACTION/STRATEGY:

ANXIETY LEVEL AFTER (1–10):

TIME: FEELING: INTENSITY (1–10):

SITUATION:

REACTION/STRATEGY:

ANXIETY LEVEL AFTER (1–10):

Self-Care

HOURS SLEPT:

NOURISHMENT (1-10):

WATER:

PHYSICAL ACTIVITY:

OTHER:

IMPACT ON MOOD (Y/N):

Today, I am grateful for:

WHAT HAPPENED TODAY

TIME: FEELING: INTENSITY (1–10):

SITUATION:

REACTION/STRATEGY:

ANXIETY LEVEL AFTER (1–10):

TIME: FEELING: INTENSITY (1–10):

SITUATION:

REACTION/STRATEGY:

ANXIETY LEVEL AFTER (1–10):

TIME: FEELING: INTENSITY (1–10):

SITUATION:

REACTION/STRATEGY:

ANXIETY LEVEL AFTER (1–10):

Self-Care

HOURS SLEPT:

NOURISHMENT (1-10):

WATER:

PHYSICAL ACTIVITY:

OTHER:

IMPACT ON MOOD (Y/N):

Today, I am grateful for:

WHAT HAPPENED TODAY

M| D| Y|

TIME: FEELING: INTENSITY (1–10):

SITUATION:

REACTION/STRATEGY:

ANXIETY LEVEL AFTER (1–10):

TIME: FEELING: INTENSITY (1–10):

SITUATION:

REACTION/STRATEGY:

ANXIETY LEVEL AFTER (1–10):

TIME: FEELING: INTENSITY (1–10):

SITUATION:

REACTION/STRATEGY:

ANXIETY LEVEL AFTER (1–10):

Self-Care

HOURS SLEPT:

NOURISHMENT (1-10):

WATER:

PHYSICAL ACTIVITY:

OTHER:

IMPACT ON MOOD (Y/N):

Today, I am grateful for:

| M| | D| | Y| |

WHAT HAPPENED TODAY

TIME: FEELING: INTENSITY (1–10):

SITUATION:

REACTION/STRATEGY:

ANXIETY LEVEL AFTER (1–10):

TIME: FEELING: INTENSITY (1–10):

SITUATION:

REACTION/STRATEGY:

ANXIETY LEVEL AFTER (1–10):

TIME: FEELING: INTENSITY (1–10):

SITUATION:

REACTION/STRATEGY:

ANXIETY LEVEL AFTER (1–10):

Self-Care

HOURS SLEPT:

NOURISHMENT (1-10):

WATER:

PHYSICAL ACTIVITY:

OTHER:

IMPACT ON MOOD (Y/N):

Today, I am grateful for:

WHAT HAPPENED TODAY

M| D| Y|

TIME: FEELING: INTENSITY (1–10):

SITUATION:

REACTION/STRATEGY:

ANXIETY LEVEL AFTER (1–10):

TIME: FEELING: INTENSITY (1–10):

SITUATION:

REACTION/STRATEGY:

ANXIETY LEVEL AFTER (1–10):

TIME: FEELING: INTENSITY (1–10):

SITUATION:

REACTION/STRATEGY:

ANXIETY LEVEL AFTER (1–10):

Self-Care

HOURS SLEPT:

NOURISHMENT (1-10):

WATER:

PHYSICAL ACTIVITY:

OTHER:

IMPACT ON MOOD (Y/N):

Today, I am grateful for:

| M| | D| | Y| |

WHAT HAPPENED TODAY

TIME: FEELING: INTENSITY (1–10):

SITUATION:

REACTION/STRATEGY:

ANXIETY LEVEL AFTER (1–10):

TIME: FEELING: INTENSITY (1–10):

SITUATION:

REACTION/STRATEGY:

ANXIETY LEVEL AFTER (1–10):

TIME: FEELING: INTENSITY (1–10):

SITUATION:

REACTION/STRATEGY:

ANXIETY LEVEL AFTER (1–10):

Self-Care

HOURS SLEPT:

NOURISHMENT (1-10):

WATER:

PHYSICAL ACTIVITY:

OTHER:

IMPACT ON MOOD (Y/N):

Today, I am grateful for:

WHAT HAPPENED TODAY

M| D| Y|

TIME: .... FEELING: .... INTENSITY (1–10): ....

SITUATION: ....

REACTION/STRATEGY: ....

ANXIETY LEVEL AFTER (1–10): ....

TIME: .... FEELING: .... INTENSITY (1–10): ....

SITUATION: ....

REACTION/STRATEGY: ....

ANXIETY LEVEL AFTER (1–10): ....

TIME: .... FEELING: .... INTENSITY (1–10): ....

SITUATION: ....

REACTION/STRATEGY: ....

ANXIETY LEVEL AFTER (1–10): ....

Self-Care

HOURS SLEPT: ....

NOURISHMENT (1-10): ....

WATER: ....

PHYSICAL ACTIVITY: ....

OTHER: ....

IMPACT ON MOOD (Y/N): ....

Today, I am grateful for:

M| D| Y|

TIME: FEELING: INTENSITY (1–10):

SITUATION:

REACTION/STRATEGY:

ANXIETY LEVEL AFTER (1–10):

TIME: FEELING: INTENSITY (1–10):

SITUATION:

REACTION/STRATEGY:

ANXIETY LEVEL AFTER (1–10):

TIME: FEELING: INTENSITY (1–10):

SITUATION:

REACTION/STRATEGY:

ANXIETY LEVEL AFTER (1–10):

Self-Care

HOURS SLEPT:

NOURISHMENT (1–10):

WATER:

PHYSICAL ACTIVITY:

OTHER:

IMPACT ON MOOD (Y/N):

Today, I am grateful for:

WHAT HAPPENED TODAY

M| D| Y|

TIME: FEELING: INTENSITY (1-10):

SITUATION:

REACTION/STRATEGY:

ANXIETY LEVEL AFTER (1-10):

TIME: FEELING: INTENSITY (1-10):

SITUATION:

REACTION/STRATEGY:

ANXIETY LEVEL AFTER (1-10):

TIME: FEELING: INTENSITY (1-10):

SITUATION:

REACTION/STRATEGY:

ANXIETY LEVEL AFTER (1-10):

Self-Care

HOURS SLEPT:

NOURISHMENT (1-10):

WATER:

PHYSICAL ACTIVITY:

OTHER:

IMPACT ON MOOD (Y/N):

Today, I am grateful for:

| M| | D| | Y| |

WHAT HAPPENED TODAY

TIME: FEELING: INTENSITY (1–10):

SITUATION:

REACTION/STRATEGY:

ANXIETY LEVEL AFTER (1–10):

TIME: FEELING: INTENSITY (1–10):

SITUATION:

REACTION/STRATEGY:

ANXIETY LEVEL AFTER (1–10):

TIME: FEELING: INTENSITY (1–10):

SITUATION:

REACTION/STRATEGY:

ANXIETY LEVEL AFTER (1–10):

Self-Care

HOURS SLEPT:

NOURISHMENT (1-10):

WATER:

PHYSICAL ACTIVITY:

OTHER:

IMPACT ON MOOD (Y/N):

Today, I am grateful for:

WHAT HAPPENED TODAY

M| D| Y|

TIME: FEELING: INTENSITY (1–10):

SITUATION:

REACTION/STRATEGY:

ANXIETY LEVEL AFTER (1–10):

TIME: FEELING: INTENSITY (1–10):

SITUATION:

REACTION/STRATEGY:

ANXIETY LEVEL AFTER (1–10):

TIME: FEELING: INTENSITY (1–10):

SITUATION:

REACTION/STRATEGY:

ANXIETY LEVEL AFTER (1–10):

Self-Care

HOURS SLEPT:

NOURISHMENT (1-10):

WATER:

PHYSICAL ACTIVITY:

OTHER:

IMPACT ON MOOD (Y/N):

Today, I am grateful for:

WHAT HAPPENED TODAY

TIME: FEELING: INTENSITY (1–10):

SITUATION:

REACTION/STRATEGY:

ANXIETY LEVEL AFTER (1–10):

TIME: FEELING: INTENSITY (1–10):

SITUATION:

REACTION/STRATEGY:

ANXIETY LEVEL AFTER (1–10):

TIME: FEELING: INTENSITY (1–10):

SITUATION:

REACTION/STRATEGY:

ANXIETY LEVEL AFTER (1–10):

Self-Care

HOURS SLEPT:

NOURISHMENT (1-10):

WATER:

PHYSICAL ACTIVITY:

OTHER:

IMPACT ON MOOD (Y/N):

Today, I am grateful for:

WHAT HAPPENED TODAY

M| D| Y|

TIME: FEELING: INTENSITY (1–10):

SITUATION:

REACTION/STRATEGY:

ANXIETY LEVEL AFTER (1–10):

TIME: FEELING: INTENSITY (1–10):

SITUATION:

REACTION/STRATEGY:

ANXIETY LEVEL AFTER (1–10):

TIME: FEELING: INTENSITY (1–10):

SITUATION:

REACTION/STRATEGY:

ANXIETY LEVEL AFTER (1–10):

Self-Care

HOURS SLEPT:

NOURISHMENT (1-10):

WATER:

PHYSICAL ACTIVITY:

OTHER:

IMPACT ON MOOD (Y/N):

Today, I am grateful for:

WHAT HAPPENED TODAY

TIME: FEELING: INTENSITY (1–10):

SITUATION:

REACTION/STRATEGY:

ANXIETY LEVEL AFTER (1–10):

TIME: FEELING: INTENSITY (1–10):

SITUATION:

REACTION/STRATEGY:

ANXIETY LEVEL AFTER (1–10):

TIME: FEELING: INTENSITY (1–10):

SITUATION:

REACTION/STRATEGY:

ANXIETY LEVEL AFTER (1–10):

Self-Care

HOURS SLEPT:

NOURISHMENT (1-10):

WATER:

PHYSICAL ACTIVITY:

OTHER:

IMPACT ON MOOD (Y/N):

Today, I am grateful for:

WHAT HAPPENED TODAY

M| D| Y|

TIME: FEELING: INTENSITY (1–10):

SITUATION:

REACTION/STRATEGY:

ANXIETY LEVEL AFTER (1–10):

TIME: FEELING: INTENSITY (1–10):

SITUATION:

REACTION/STRATEGY:

ANXIETY LEVEL AFTER (1–10):

TIME: FEELING: INTENSITY (1–10):

SITUATION:

REACTION/STRATEGY:

ANXIETY LEVEL AFTER (1–10):

Self-Care

HOURS SLEPT:

NOURISHMENT (1-10):

WATER:

PHYSICAL ACTIVITY:

OTHER:

IMPACT ON MOOD (Y/N):

Today, I am grateful for:

WHAT HAPPENED TODAY

TIME:　　　　　　FEELING:　　　　　　　　　　　　INTENSITY (1–10):

SITUATION:

REACTION/STRATEGY:

ANXIETY LEVEL AFTER (1–10):

TIME:　　　　　　FEELING:　　　　　　　　　　　　INTENSITY (1–10):

SITUATION:

REACTION/STRATEGY:

ANXIETY LEVEL AFTER (1–10):

TIME:　　　　　　FEELING:　　　　　　　　　　　　INTENSITY (1–10):

SITUATION:

REACTION/STRATEGY:

ANXIETY LEVEL AFTER (1–10):

Self-Care

HOURS SLEPT:

NOURISHMENT (1-10):

WATER:

PHYSICAL ACTIVITY:

OTHER:

IMPACT ON MOOD (Y/N):

Today, I am grateful for:

WHAT HAPPENED TODAY

M| D| Y|

TIME: FEELING: INTENSITY (1-10):

SITUATION:

REACTION/STRATEGY:

ANXIETY LEVEL AFTER (1-10):

TIME: FEELING: INTENSITY (1-10):

SITUATION:

REACTION/STRATEGY:

ANXIETY LEVEL AFTER (1-10):

TIME: FEELING: INTENSITY (1-10):

SITUATION:

REACTION/STRATEGY:

ANXIETY LEVEL AFTER (1-10):

Self-Care

HOURS SLEPT:

NOURISHMENT (1-10):

WATER:

PHYSICAL ACTIVITY:

OTHER:

IMPACT ON MOOD (Y/N):

Today, I am grateful for:

M|	D|	Y|

WHAT HAPPENED TODAY

TIME: FEELING: INTENSITY (1–10):

SITUATION:

REACTION/STRATEGY:

ANXIETY LEVEL AFTER (1–10):

TIME: FEELING: INTENSITY (1–10):

SITUATION:

REACTION/STRATEGY:

ANXIETY LEVEL AFTER (1–10):

TIME: FEELING: INTENSITY (1–10):

SITUATION:

REACTION/STRATEGY:

ANXIETY LEVEL AFTER (1–10):

Self-Care

HOURS SLEPT:

NOURISHMENT (1-10):

WATER:

PHYSICAL ACTIVITY:

OTHER:

IMPACT ON MOOD (Y/N):

Today, I am grateful for:

WHAT HAPPENED TODAY

M| D| Y|

TIME: FEELING: INTENSITY (1–10):

SITUATION:

REACTION/STRATEGY:

ANXIETY LEVEL AFTER (1–10):

TIME: FEELING: INTENSITY (1–10):

SITUATION:

REACTION/STRATEGY:

ANXIETY LEVEL AFTER (1–10):

TIME: FEELING: INTENSITY (1–10):

SITUATION:

REACTION/STRATEGY:

ANXIETY LEVEL AFTER (1–10):

Self-Care

HOURS SLEPT:

NOURISHMENT (1-10):

WATER:

PHYSICAL ACTIVITY:

OTHER:

IMPACT ON MOOD (Y/N):

Today, I am grateful for:

| M| | D| | Y| | **WHAT HAPPENED TODAY** |

TIME: FEELING: INTENSITY (1–10):

SITUATION:

REACTION/STRATEGY:

ANXIETY LEVEL AFTER (1–10):

TIME: FEELING: INTENSITY (1–10):

SITUATION:

REACTION/STRATEGY:

ANXIETY LEVEL AFTER (1–10):

TIME: FEELING: INTENSITY (1–10):

SITUATION:

REACTION/STRATEGY:

ANXIETY LEVEL AFTER (1–10):

Self-Care

HOURS SLEPT:

NOURISHMENT (1-10):

WATER:

PHYSICAL ACTIVITY:

OTHER:

IMPACT ON MOOD (Y/N):

Today, I am grateful for:

WHAT HAPPENED TODAY

M| D| Y|

TIME: FEELING: INTENSITY (1–10):

SITUATION:

REACTION/STRATEGY:

ANXIETY LEVEL AFTER (1–10):

TIME: FEELING: INTENSITY (1–10):

SITUATION:

REACTION/STRATEGY:

ANXIETY LEVEL AFTER (1–10):

TIME: FEELING: INTENSITY (1–10):

SITUATION:

REACTION/STRATEGY:

ANXIETY LEVEL AFTER (1–10):

Self-Care

HOURS SLEPT:

NOURISHMENT (1-10):

WATER:

PHYSICAL ACTIVITY:

OTHER:

IMPACT ON MOOD (Y/N):

Today, I am grateful for:

| M| | D| | Y| |

WHAT HAPPENED TODAY

TIME: FEELING: INTENSITY (1–10):

SITUATION:

REACTION/STRATEGY:

ANXIETY LEVEL AFTER (1–10):

TIME: FEELING: INTENSITY (1–10):

SITUATION:

REACTION/STRATEGY:

ANXIETY LEVEL AFTER (1–10):

TIME: FEELING: INTENSITY (1–10):

SITUATION:

REACTION/STRATEGY:

ANXIETY LEVEL AFTER (1–10):

Self-Care

HOURS SLEPT:

NOURISHMENT (1-10):

WATER:

PHYSICAL ACTIVITY:

OTHER:

IMPACT ON MOOD (Y/N):

Today, I am grateful for:

Average Anxiety Level

① ② ③ ④ ⑤ ⑥ ⑦ ⑧ ⑨ ⑩

2 Most Common Feelings

....

↓   WHAT LED UP TO THE FEELING   ↓

....

....

↓   STRATEGIES THAT WORKED OR DIDN'T WORK   ↓

↑ ↓ ↔ ....   ↑ ↓ ↔ ....

↑ ↓ ↔ ....   ↑ ↓ ↔ ....

↑ ↓ ↔ ....   ↑ ↓ ↔ ....

Self-Care That Helped Overall Mental Health

↑ ↓ ↔ ....

↑ ↓ ↔ ....

↑ ↓ ↔ ....

For Next Month

I WANT TO FOCUS ON CHANGING ONE THING:

....

....

THIS IS HOW I'LL DO IT:

....

....

Other Notes and Observations

Hi there,

We hope using *Mental Health Tracker* helped you. If you have any questions or concerns about your book, or have received a damaged copy, please contact customerservice@penguinrandomhouse.com. We're here and happy to help.

Also, please consider writing a review on your favorite retailer's website to let others know what you thought of the book.

Sincerely,
The Zeitgeist Team